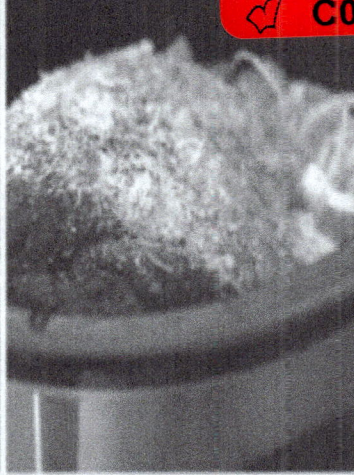

AIR FRYER
COOKBOOK FOR BEGINNERS

The complete Beginners guide To Healthy, Quick & Easy Air Fried **HOMEMADE MEALS**. Delicious Recipes To Fry, Grill, Roast and Bake For Smart People

DUNCAN ROWLAND

AIR FRYER COOKBOOK FOR BEGINNERS

The Complete Beginners Guide To Healthy, Quick & Easy Air Fried HOMEMADE MEALS. Delicious Recipes To Fry, Grill, Roast And Bake For Smart People

DUNCAN ROWLAND

Table of Contents

Air Fryer

Breakfast Recipes

1. Apple Fritters Prepared with an Air Fryer
2. Crispy Breakfast Burritos Prepared in an Air Fryer
3. Air Fryer Donuts
4. Cups of French toast cooked in an air fryer, topped with raspberries
5. Scotch Eggs Prepared in an Air Fryer
6. Croquettes for breakfast made in the air fryer with eggs and asparagus
7. Air Fryer Breakfast Sweet Potato Skins
8. Cookies Prepared with an Air Fryer
9. Candied Bacon Finished In the Air Fryer
10. Cheesy Breakfast Egg Rolls
11. The Banana Bread Pizza Made In the Air Fryer
12. Air-Fried Ham and Egg Pockets in the Air Fryer
13. Mini Nutella Doughnut Holes Made with an Air Fryer
14. Bourbon bacon cooked in an air fryer
15. Sticks of French toast cooked in an air fryer
16. Air-Fryer Red Potatoes
17. Puff Pastry Danishes Baked in an Air Fryer

Lunch Recipes

18. The Ultimate Spinach and Artichoke Dip
19. Caviar
20. Broccoli cheese soup
21. Homemade Chicken Apple Sausage
22. The Very Best Cinnamon Rolls
23. Chickpea Tot Hot dish
24. Quick BBQ Sausage Sloppy Joes
25. Crepes that Have Been Folded, Filled with Smoked Ham, and Topped with Butter
26. Open "Face" Egg Salad Sandwiches
27. Pimento Grilled Cheese
28. Kid-Friendly Pizzadillas
29. Salad made with creamy chicken

- Hawaiian Plate Lunch with Macaroni Salad 30
- Air Fryer Broccoli 31
- Air Fryer Brussels sprouts 32

Dinner Recipes

- Cajun Air Fryer Salmon Two salmon fillets 33
- Mexican-Style Stuffed Chicken Breasts Prepared in an Air Fryer 34
- Turkey Breast Prepared in an Air Fryer 35
- Baby Back Ribs Cooked in an Air Fryer 36
- Meatloaf 37
- Breaded Pork Chops Cooked in an Air Fryer 38
- AIR FRIED TERIYAKI PORK CHOPS 39
- Air-Fried Chicken Fajitas in the Air Fryer 40
- Air Fryer Honey Garlic Chicken Wings 41
- Air Fryer Swai Fish 42
- Ribeye Steak 43
- Lobster Tails for the Air Fryer 44
- Air Fryer BBQ Chicken Wings 45
- Chicken Parmesan 45
- Buffalo Chicken Wings Baked In the Air Fryer 46
- Chicken Street Tacos Made In the Air Fryer 47
- Parmesan-Crusted Chicken Done In the Air Fryer 49
- Pistachio-Crusted Chicken Prepared In an Air Fryer 50
- Chicken Prepared In an Air Fryer 52
- Air Fryer Honey Mustard Salmon 53
- Taco Casserole Made In the Air Fryer 54
- Catfish cooked in an air fryer 55
- Nachos Prepared in an Air Fryer 56
- Air Fryer Steak Kabobs 57
- Chicken Breasts Prepared in an Air Fryer 58
- Pork Chops Cooked In an Air Fryer 60
- Pickles Prepared in an Air Fryer 61
- Air-Fryer Chicken Wings 62
- Garlic Bread Prepared in an Air Fryer 63
- 64
- 64
- 66
- 68
- 69
- 69
- 70
- 70
- 71
- 72
- 73
- 74
- 75
- 76
- 77
- 79
- 81
- 82
- 83
- 84

Air-Fryer Shrimp in a Sauce Made of Coconut and Apricots	53
Air-Fried Spinach and Feta	54
Avocado Cut into Wedge Shapes Wrapped In Bacon	55
Zucchini Pizza Fritters	66
Mushroom Roll-Ups Prepared in an Air Fryer	67
Thai Meatballs with Chicken	68
Shrimp Cake Sliders Prepared in an Air Fryer	69
Calamari Prepared in an Air Fryer	70
Samosas	71
Air-Fryer Spicy Ginger Beef Skewers	72
Buffalo Bites	73
Air-Fryer French Fries	74
Air-Fryer Spring Rolls with a Crispy Sriracha Sauce	75
Air-Fryer Fiesta Chicken Fingers	76
Air-Fryer Cheeseburger Onion Rings	77
Garlic-Rosemary Brussels Sprouts Prepared in an Air Fryer	78
Quinoa Arancini Prepared with an Air Fryer	84
Air-Fried Meatballs Stuffed with Figs and Goat Cheese	85
Empanadas	86
Components of an Air-Fried Ravioli Dish	87
Air-Fryer Taquitos	88
Air-Fried Cauliflower	89
Nashville Hot Chicken Prepared in an Air Fryer	90
Beef Wellington Wontons Prepared in an Air Fryer	91
Air Fryer Pumpkin Fries	92
Hot Meatballs Prepared in an Air Fryer	94
Mini Chimichangas Prepared in an Air Fryer	95
Beefy Swiss Bundles Prepared in an Air Fryer	96
Air-Fried Drumsticks with a Crispy Curry Finish	97
	98
	99
	100
	101
	102
	103
	104
	105
	106
	108
	109
	110
	111
	112
	113
	114

Air Fryer

The air fryer is just a countertop convection oven that has been cranked up; it does not cook the food. (However, it is important to bear in mind that baking and air-frying are not the same things.) The compact kitchen device, which was developed and patented by Philips Electronics Company, makes the bold claim that it can replicate the outcomes of deep-frying using just hot air and very little or no oil at all.

This kitchen appliance has had a meteoric rise in popularity over the last few years; as of July 2020, about forty percent of houses in the United States owned one. You may air-fry a wide variety of foods, ranging from frozen chicken wings and handmade French fries to roasted veggies and freshly baked cookies.

How exactly do air fryers prepare food?

The heating mechanism and fan of an air fryer are located in the upper area of the appliance. When the device is turned on, the food is placed in a basket similar to a fryer, and hot air is then forced down onto and around the food. This quick circulation causes the food to become crisp, like that of deep frying but without the use of oil.

The following is a guide on how to operate an air fryer:

1. Put all of your groceries into the basket.

The capacity of the basket may range anywhere from 2 to 10 quarts, depending on the size of your air fryer. In most circumstances, you will need to add one or two tablespoons of oil to the dish to assist it in becoming beautiful and crispy. If you're in a rush, you may make cleaning in an air fryer a little bit simpler by placing foil in the appliance beforehand.

2. Adjust the time and the temperature to your liking.

Cooking periods and temperatures in an air fryer normally run anywhere from five to twenty-five minutes at temperatures between three hundred fifty and four hundred degrees Fahrenheit, depending on the item being prepared.

3. Give the dish time to cook.

If you want the food to crisp up equally, you may need to flip or turn it halfway through the cooking period. This will help it brown more evenly. You must clean your air fryer once you have finished cooking in it.

Do you want to know how to make air-fried food that is brown and golden in color? We have advice for using an air fryer that will help every dish turn out flawlessly, as well as common blunders that you should try to avoid making while using an air fryer.

Which brands make the most effective air fryers?

To determine which model is the greatest air fryer, our Test Kitchen put a number of different models through their paces, and the results showed that three brands came out on top. Since its release, the Philips Avance TurboStar Air Fryer has been a favorite of ours here at Best Buy. Our team of experts also found the Black &

There is a wide variety of prices for these electronic devices since the size and functionality vary. You should consider purchasing some air fryer accessories in addition to the device itself if you want to use the appliance.

What kinds of foods may be prepared in an air fryer?

Although the majority of the finest recipes for an air fryer include items that are traditionally fried in oil, you can also use this kitchen device to roast vegetables, bake cookies, and cook meat.

Frozen Finger Foods

When it comes to the preparation of frozen dishes that are supposed to have a fried flavor, the air fryer is a star performer. You may prepare a wide variety of frozen delicacies by using the air fryer, like chicken nuggets, mozzarella sticks, and frozen French fries, to name a few.

Homemade Finger Foods

Try creating air-fryer sweet potato fries, air-fryer pickles, or air-fryer potato chips if you want to prepare your finger foods from scratch. The air fryer is a terrific alternative for preparing crispy homemade snacks and sides. Air-fryer appetizers like air-fryer ravioli and air-fryer egg rolls are quite addictive, so make sure you don't miss out on them.

On the other hand, mozzarella sticks prepared from frozen mozzarella that has been air-fried are excellent, while fresh mozzarella turns into a gloppy mess (so homemade cheese curds are out).

Chicken, fish, and other cuts of meat

You may prepare chicken in an air fryer so that it is juicy and tender. You should experiment with chicken recipes for the air fryer, such as air-fryer Nashville hot chicken. The keto meatballs that are prepared in an air fryer are a wonderful alternative for those looking for a healthy food option. When it comes to meals made with fish and seafood, one of our favorites is this crumb-topped sole prepared in an air fryer, as well as air-fried cod.

This excellent equipment may also be used to create reassuring dishes, such as air-fryer beef loaf and air-fryer pig loin roast, amongst other delicious options.

Roasted Vegetables

Because they are miniature versions of conventional ovens, air fryers are ideal for roasting vegetables, and this is particularly true if you are just preparing food for one or two people. Air-fried cauliflower with herbs and lemon, air-fried red potatoes, air-fried asparagus, and air-fried Brussels sprouts with garlic rosemary are some of our favorite air-fried vegetable dishes.

However, if you are going to prepare vegetables using this device, you should avoid cooking leafy greens.

Some Baked Goods

Cookies and apple fritters are just two examples of the kind of little baked products that can be made in an air fryer (here's how to make cookies in an air fryer). Air fryers may also be used to produce delicious appetizers. Make these small Nutella doughnut holes in an air fryer for a decadent treat any time of year, or try your hand at air-frying some peppermint lava cakes for the winter holidays. Air-fryer recipes for breakfast that are worth trying include air-fryer bourbon bacon cinnamon buns and air-fryer French toast sticks. Don't forget to use the air fryer when it's time to prepare the first meal of the day.

Which one should I go with according to the total number of people in my family?

The air fryer is just one example of how technological advancements over the years have led to improvements in various types of kitchen appliances. This air fryer had a heating element that ran on 120 DC volts, and it had a fan attached to the back of the unit that moved the hot air around the food while it was cooking.

Since that time, numerous improvements have been made to the fundamental design, and it wasn't until 2010 that Philips released the world's first contemporary air fryer. This air fryer was a game-changer in the world of cooking because it allowed food to be prepared more quickly and with less oil than traditional methods required.

It goes without saying that the industry took on rapidly, and as a result, there are a great many brands, manufacturers, and sizes of air fryers available today.

The modern consumer is faced with an overwhelming number of options, making it difficult for them to make a decision. Your first order of business should be determining the maximum capacity of the air fryer that will meet your needs.

Which one to select is dependent on the size of the family

Modern technology has enhanced kitchen equipment throughout the years, and the air fryer is no exception. This air fryer used a 120 DC volt heating source and a fan on the rear of the appliance to pump hot air over the food.

This initial concept has undergone several revisions since then, with Philips introducing the first contemporary air fryer in 2010. This air fryer revolutionized the kitchen world by frying food quicker and simpler while using less oil. Needless to say, the industry rapidly took on, and there are now several types, manufacturers, and sizes of air fryers available.

Consumers are today pampered with so many options that it may be difficult to choose. The first thing you should think about is what size capacity air fryer is right for you.

The capacity of an air fryer

Choosing Air Fryer Dimensions

When choosing the size of your air fryer, the following things should be taken into account:

If you're seeking an alternate cooking technique to rapidly reheat food and produce light meals throughout the day, a smaller air fryer would suffice.

However, if you want to use it to cook whole meals, you should determine if you need a larger air fryer based on the following questions. How many people do you prepare for daily, and how enormous are their appetites?

Here's a basic rundown of the various sizes:

- 1-2 individuals: A little air fryer (1 to 3 quarts) (0.95 to 2.8 Liters).
- 3-4 people: A 4-to-6-quart family-sized air fryer (3.8 to 5.7 Liters).
- 5 to 6 people: An extra-large air fryer with a capacity of 7 to 8 quarts (6.6 to 7.6 Liters).
- 7-9 individuals: A multifunctional air fryer with a capacity ranging from 9 to 30 quarts (3.5 to 28.4 Liters).

The amount of counter space available in your kitchen.

You may be tempted to buy a larger air fryer than you need, but keep in mind that larger air fryers may take up a lot of countertop space. The last thing you want to do is move the air fryer from a cabinet to the countertop and back again.

What are your dietary requirements and preferences?

If you want meat on the bone that is irregular in form and hefty, you may need a larger air fryer so that it can fit in the basket.

Small air fryers typically have a meal capacity of 1 to 3 Quarts (0.95 to 2.8 Liters). In one cooking session, the 1 Quart (0.95 Liters) air fryers should be able to accommodate 1 small chicken breast with some fries on the side. On average, the 2 to 3 Quarts (1.9 to 2.8 Liters) air fryers can cook 2 chicken breasts or 4-6 chicken wings in a single cooking session.

Small air fryers are ideal for producing fast and simple no-mess snacks and light dinners. They are also an excellent alternative to the microwave for reheating meals since they heat up rapidly while keeping the food moist on the inside.

A smaller air fryer is generally the best choice for single persons or those who only cook for one or two people at a time since it saves countertop space.

In one cooking session, the 4 to 5 Quarts (3.8 to 4.7 Litres) air fryers should contain 4 chicken breasts or half a package of frozen chips. This is an excellent serving size for 3 to 4 people for daily meals, but if your appetite is a little greater, you may want to choose a 6 Quarts (5.7 Litres) air fryer. Overcrowding the basket may result in uneven cooking and food that is not fully cooked on the inside.

Most 6 Quart (5.7 liters) air fryers can cook an entire chicken or a whole bag of frozen chips in a single cooking session. This size air fryer also has additional functionality, so you can cook a variety of foods with it (depending on the model and make).

Any of the air fryers in this range would be sufficient for a family of 3 to 4 people, however, depending on your appetite and the sorts of food you prepare for your regular meals, you may choose the 6 Quart (5.7 Liters) basket.

Air Fryer with Extra Large Capacity

Larger households of 5 to 6 people might consider purchasing an extra-large air fryer. These air fryers have a capacity of 7 to 8 quarts (6.6 to 7.6 Liters). They can hold a complete chicken (approximately 3 pounds or 1.3 kilograms), 23 chicken wings, or two bags of frozen fries.

The quantity of pre-set programs that come with this larger capacity air fryer is another advantage. Air fry, bake, grill, roast, reheat, dehydrate, and toast are the most common pre-sets. This makes it very user-friendly since you can just place your food in the air fryer and cook it with a single touch.

Air Fryers with Multiple Functions

The capacity of this Air Fryer with Rotisserie function is 15.5 Quarts (14.7 Liters)!

What Size Air Fryer Should You Purchase?

Small air fryers: These are suitable for singles or couples who want to reheat and prepare small meals.

Air fryers for families of 3 to 4 people: This size is adequate for households where the air fryers are used often to make meals.

Extra Large air fryers: Best for huge households of 5 or 6 people and the air fryer will be used for everyday meals.

Multifunctional air fryers: These should be considered if you often serve 7 or more people.

After you've determined the size category and intended usage, think about things like countertop space and dietary demands and preferences. Take a look at our evaluations for each of these categories to help you pick the finest air fryer for you. This is where you may further restrict your search.

We hope that this has aided you in deciding on the finest air fryer for you.

How to Use and Clean It Properly

Air fryers have experienced a big spike in popularity among home cooks in recent years, and it's simple to understand why. These simple compact kitchen equipment make it simple to cook a fast supper. Air fryers remove moisture from meals by employing heated air containing fine oil droplets, efficiently eliminating the high-fat and high-calorie oils. Since air fryers utilize a quarter of the oil to cook dishes, you'll end up with lower-calorie items far more rapidly than conventional cooking techniques.

Because of these advantages, home chefs prefer to use their air fryers more often than their other equipment, necessitating regular cleaning. But, it might be tough to determine whether they are cleaning it in the best manner possible.

After each usage, you should clean your air fryer. Because it employs tiny oil droplets to cook the food, grease and oil build-up will ultimately accumulate in the machine. If you let too much build up, your air fryer will ultimately heat food less effectively, spend more energy, and need much more rigorous cleaning to remove the built-up particles. If you clean it after each use, it will prevent oil and dirt from harming the performance of your machine.

That being said, we recognize that cleaning your air fryer after each usage isn't feasible, particularly if you live a busy life. A gentle wipe-down of the basket with a damp or dry paper towel or washcloth would enough for a fast clean. Alternatively, you can just place your air fryer basket in the dishwasher for a hands-free, time-saving alternative. Additionally, we suggest scrubbing the interior of the air fryer, with the basket removed, at least every 5 uses depending on what sorts of food you are frying. This helps prevent loose particles and crumbs from moving near the heating element and from liquids and greases baking in hard-to-reach locations.

Cleaning Your Air Fryer

Follow the steps outlined below to ensure that your air fryer is fully cleaned and sanitized after use.

- Unplug your air fryer
- Allow the air fryer components to cool to room temperature if you have recently fried.
- Take out the basket.
- Let the basket soak in warm water and soap for 10-15 minutes
- If there's caked-on grease or hard-to-remove stains in the basket, try cleaning with a non-abrasive brush with warm water and soap solution still in the basket
- Clean the inside of the air fryer with a moist cloth or sponge and a tiny bit of dish soap.
- Wipe clean the heating element with a sponge or cloth after turning the air fryer upside down.
- To remove obstinate residue, create a mixture of baking soda and water and scrub with a soft-bristled brush.
- Allow your air fryer components to completely dry before reassembling.

Is there anything you should avoid using an air fryer for?

West advises taking extra care of the nonstick coating within your air fryer. It's also vital to avoid using metal utensils inside the air fryer when preparing or cooking, in addition to utilizing nonabrasive cleaning equipment. Food will adhere to the components considerably more if the coating is destroyed, so be cautious. She also mentions that each air fryer is different and that you should always use a recipe as a reference for duration and temperature. This can help you prevent burnt-on messes that will need a thorough cleaning.

Health Advantages

When you bite into a dish of French fries or a platter of fried chicken, the familiar, crispy crunchy and moist, chewy middle strike you immediately away.

However, the tempting flavor of fried dishes comes at a cost. The oils used to prepare them have been linked to health issues such as heart disease, type 2 diabetes, and cancer. Enter air fryers, which promise the flavor, texture, and golden-brown color of oil-fried dishes without the fat and calories. But do these deep fryer substitutes live up to their claims?

How Do They Function?

Air fryers are square or egg-shaped gadgets that sit on your counter, roughly the size of a coffeemaker. You place the food to be fried (chopped potatoes, chicken nuggets, zucchini slices) in a slide-out basket. You may cover it lightly with oil if you desire. A fan circulates hot air (up to 400 degrees Fahrenheit) over the meal. It's similar to a convection oven.

The flowing air cooks the exterior of the meals first, creating a crispy brown coating while keeping the interior soft, similar to deep-fried delicacies. A container underneath the basket collects any oil that falls while the food cooks.

- Chicken, including nuggets and fingers
- Vegetables
- French fries with onion rings
- Sticks of cheese
- Fish
- Pizza
- Doughnuts

Some versions additionally have toast and bake functions, making them more equivalent to standard ovens. These may be used to make brownies or roast a bird. One disadvantage of many of these appliances is their limited basket size, which makes it difficult to prepare a complete family dinner.

This cooking technique may help reduce some of the other negative impacts of oil frying. When you cook potatoes or other starchy meals, the chemical acrylamide is formed, which studies have linked to an increased risk of cancer. According to one research, air frying reduces the level of acrylamide in fried potatoes by 90%.

How to Use an Air Fryer

Aside from being a healthier option to a deep fryer, an air fryer may save you time in the kitchen by reducing cooking and cleaning time. However, here are some health-conscious precautions to remember while using an air fryer:

Most air fryers need at least five inches of clearance above the exhaust vent. Otherwise, they pose a fire risk.

Use just a little quantity of oil: Toss or brush each dish of food with one to two tablespoons of oil. Too much oil not only increases calorie and fat content, but may also encourage smoking, make meals taste terrible, and hurt your health by releasing free radicals that can injure cells.

Avoid using aerosol sprays: Aerosol cooking oils can degrade the nonstick basket of an air fryer, generating hazardous fumes.

While air fryers are fantastic, alternate your cooking techniques throughout the week by sautéing, slow cooking, and steaming. This will minimize your exposure to toxins such as acrylamide even more. It also guarantees that you eat a broader range of meals, not simply those suitable with air fryers, broadening the spectrum of nutrients you ingest.

Breakfast Recipes

Apple Fritters Prepared with an Air Fryer

Preparation time: 15 minutes   **Cooking time:** 20 minutes   **Serving:** 2

Nutrition:

- Calories: 500
- Carbs: 23g
- Protein: 8g
- Fats: 0g

Ingredients

- 1 and 1/2 cups of flour for all purposes
- 1/4 cup sugar
- 2 teaspoons of powdered baking soda
- 1-and-a-half milligrams of ground cinnamon
- 1/2 teaspoon salt
- 2/3 cup 2% milk
- 2 large eggs, room temperature
- 1 tablespoon lemon juice
- 1-and-a-half teaspoons of vanilla extract, split between two Honeycrisp apples that are medium in size and have been peeled and chopped
- Cooking spray
- 14 of a cup of butter
- 1 fluid ounce of confectioner's sugar
- 1 tablespoon 2% milk

Directions

1. Bring the temperature of the air fryer to 410 degrees. Flour, sugar, baking powder, cinnamon, and salt should all be mixed in a large bowl. Add milk, eggs, lemon juice, and 1 teaspoon of vanilla extract; stir just until moistened. Mix in some apples.
2. Spray the air fryer basket with cooking spray and line it with parchment paper that has been cut to fit. On a piece of parchment, drop portions of the dough measuring 1/4 cup at a distance of 2 inches apart in batches. Spray with some kind of cooking spray. Cook for another 5 or 6 minutes, until the meat, is golden brown. Fry the fritters in the air for an additional one to two minutes, until they are golden brown.
3. In a small saucepan set over medium-high heat, butter should be melted. Cook while paying careful attention for approximately 5 minutes, or until the butter begins to brown and froth. Take the pan off the heat, and let it cool somewhat. After the butter has been browned, add the confectioners' sugar, the remaining 1 tablespoon of milk, and the remaining 1/2 teaspoon of vanilla essence and stir until creamy. Drizzle over the fritters before serving.

Preparation time: 10 minutes   **cooking time:** 20 minutes   **Serving:** 2

Nutrition:

- Calories: 2550
- Carbs: 380g
- Protein: 300g
- Fats: 25g

Ingredients

- (2 large or 3–4 small potatoes) of diced russet or Yukon gold potatoes, cut into pieces about half an inch
- 2 tablespoons avocado oil
- 1 teaspoon of the powdered or starchy arrowroot (optional for crispiness)
- 2 teaspoons paprika
- 1 level teaspoon of powdered garlic
- 1/2 milligrams of dried onion powder
- 1 teaspoon salt
- 1/2 milligrams of ground black pepper
- For the sausage made from ground pork:
- 1 pound of pork ground with the breakfast seasoning
- 1 can of green chiles, chopped, with a net weight of 4 ounces
  For the eggs to be scrambled:
- 8 big eggs, whisked
- 2 teaspoons of the milk of your choice
- 1/2 teaspoon salt & pepper
- For the burritos, you'll need:
- About one cup's worth of shredded cheddar cheese
- 7–8 burrito-size (10-inch) tortillas with spicy sauce, salsa, sour cream, etc

Directions

1. To prepare the potatoes, preheat the oven to 425 degrees Fahrenheit. The diced potatoes should be placed on a baking sheet that has either a silicone baking liner or parchment paper covering them. Put the potatoes in a large bowl and pour the oil, arrowroot powder, paprika, garlic powder, onion powder, salt, and pepper over them. Use your hands to stir everything together until the potatoes are equally covered with oil. Put the potatoes in the oven and bake for a total of 30 minutes, tossing them halfway during the baking time. While the potatoes are baking in the oven, prepare the rest of your ingredients.
2. To prepare the ground sausage, heat a pan that does not need oil or butter over medium heat. Add the ground pork and, while it is cooking, use a wooden spoon or a spatula to break up the meat into tiny pieces. Maintaining an even temperature during the cooking process, the meat should be cooked for around seven to nine minutes. Add the green chilies and toss until they are evenly distributed. Take the meat out of the pan after it is done and put it aside.

3. Prepare the eggs by lowering the heat to a medium-low setting. Eggs, milk, and seasonings like salt and pepper should be whisked together in a medium basin. Put the meat back into the pan it was cooked in and add one tablespoon of butter or ghee to the pan. After the butter has melted, add the eggs to the pan. Continue to stir the eggs with a spatula while maintaining a low temperature and do this until the eggs thicken and are fully cooked. Remove the eggs from the pan, then turn off the heat.
4. Burritos may be easily assembled by setting up an assembly station with tortillas, cooked ground sausage, scrambled eggs, and shredded cheddar cheese. Put as much as 1 and a half cups of filling in each tortilla for the entire amount. I filled each tortilla with around a half cup's worth of beef, a third cup's worth of potatoes, a quarter cup's worth of scrambled eggs, and a hefty pinch's worth of shredded cheese. Take care not to overstuff the burritos.
5. Burritos may be made by rolling tortillas and filling them into a burrito that is rolled up tightly and securely to include all of the ingredients (see pictures above to help). The first thing you need to do is pull the edges of the tortilla over the end of the filling until they are tight.
6. Cover the edges that were folded over in Step 1 by pulling the bottom of the tortilla up and over the filling using your thumbs. This should completely enclose the contents.
7. Tuck the bottom of the folded tortilla from Step 2 into the burrito. Additionally, tuck the edges of the folded tortilla from both the top and bottom of the folded tortilla. In the fourth step, fold the burrito over the open tortilla that is left over so that it covers the tucked sides and bottom.
8. Fry in an air fryer and serve: With great care, arrange two burritos within the basket of the air fryer. Fry the burritos in an air fryer at 350 degrees Fahrenheit for six to ten minutes, or until they are crisp and golden brown. Enjoy with toppings like salsa, sour cream, and various kinds of spicy sauces.
9. And then keep the burritos in an airtight container in the refrigerator for up to four days. Reheat the burritos before serving. At a temperature of 325 degrees Fahrenheit, air fried the cold burritos for 14 to 16 minutes, or until they are golden brown and crispy.
10. Prepare the burritos for the freezer and reheat them according to the instructions up to step 5, and then let them cool entirely on the counter for at least 30 minutes. Burritos may be kept in the freezer for up to three months if they are wrapped individually in plastic wrap and placed in an airtight container. Fry frozen burritos in an air fryer at 250 degrees Fahrenheit for thirty minutes while spraying them with avocado spray oil. After that, raise the temperature to 350 degrees Fahrenheit and continue air frying for two to three minutes longer, or until the burritos are crispy and golden brown.

Air Fryer Donuts

Preparation time: 15 minutes **Cooking time: 30 minutes** **Serving: 2 to 3**

Nutrition

- Calories: 238
- Carbs: 26g
- Protein: 5g
- Fats: 4g

Ingredients

- 1 cup milk, heated to a temperature of roughly 100 degrees Fahrenheit (lukewarm)
- 2 1/2 tsp. active dry yeast or quick yeast
- 1/4 cup granulated sugar
- 1/2 tsp salt
- 1 egg
- 1/4 cup unsalted butter
- Melted 3 cups all-purpose flour Oil Spray
- Coconut oil
- 2 cups of powdered sugar
- 2 teaspoons of vanilla essence
- 4 tablespoons of boiling water, according to taste

Directions

1. Mix yeast, sugar, and lukewarm milk together in the bowl of an electric stand mixer that is equipped with a dough hook. Stir the mixture very gently. Let it rest for 10 minutes until frothy (If nothing happens your milk was too hot or the yeast is too old, so start over).
2. The milk mixture should next have sugar, salt, an egg, melted butter, and two cups of flour added to it. Mix on low speed until incorporated, then with the mixer still running, gradually add the remaining cup of flour until the dough no longer adheres to the bowl. Mix on low speed until blended. Knead the dough for five minutes at medium-low speed until it is smooth and elastic, then increase the speed to medium.
3. Put the dough in a basin that has been buttered, then cover it with plastic wrap and set it aside. Allow the dough to rise in a warm area until it has doubled in size. If you press your finger into the dough and the impression is still there after a few seconds, the dough is ready to be used.
4. After turning the dough out onto a floured surface, punching it down, and rolling it out gently to a thickness of approximately half an inch, using a round cutter measuring three inches in diameter and a smaller round cutter measuring one inch in diameter, cut out ten to twelve donuts.
5. Donuts and doughnut holes should be placed on parchment paper that has been dusted with a little bit of flour and then loosely covered with greased plastic wrap. Let doughnuts rise until twice in volume, approximately 30 minutes. Heat the Air Fryer to 350 degrees Fahrenheit.
6. Spray the basket of the air fryer with oil spray, and then transfer the donuts to the basket so that they are arranged in a single layer. Donuts should be sprayed with oil spray before being cooked at 350

degrees Fahrenheit for around four minutes. Continue in this manner with the remaining donuts and holes.

7. While the donuts are cooking in the Air Fryer, melt the butter in a small skillet over medium heat in preparation for the glaze. Mix in the vanilla essence and powdered sugar until the mixture is smooth. Take the icing off the heat and, one tablespoon at a time, whisk in hot water while continuing to stir until the icing is slightly thin but not runny. Set aside.

8. Donuts and doughnut holes should be dipped in the glaze using two forks to ensure that they are well covered. Place the doughnuts on a wire rack that has been positioned over a baking sheet with a rim so that any extra glaze may drop off. Let set until glaze hardens, approximately 10 minutes.

NOTES

1. Check that the temperature of the milk is no higher than 115 degrees Fahrenheit. Utilizing a hot liquid will be fatal to the yeast.
2. If you don't have an instant-read thermometer, you may check the temperature of the milk by drizzling a few drops of it over the inside of your wrist. The temperature ought to be warm. The yeast will perish if the temperature is high, but it will stay dormant if the temperature is low.

Cups of French toast cooked in an air fryer, topped with raspberries

Preparation time: 10 minutes   Cooking time: 15 minutes   Serving: 1

Nutrition

- Calories: 410
- Carbs: 44g
- Protein: 13g
- Fats: 21g

Ingredients

- 2 slices of Italian bread, each sliced into squares about 0.5 inches on a side.
- 1/2 cup of raspberries, either fresh or frozen
- 2 ounces of cream cheese, cubed and measured to be 1/2 inch in size
- 2 big eggs
- 1/2 cup 2% milk
- 1 tablespoon maple syrup
- syrup made from raspberry:
- cornstarch equivalent to 2 tablespoons
- 13 of a cup of water
- 2 cups of raspberries, either fresh or frozen, portioned out
- 1 tablespoon lemon juice
- 1 tablespoon maple syrup
- 1/2 milligrams of grated lemon zest
- Cinnamon powder, with a possible

Directions

1. Place one-half of the bread cubes in each of the two oiled custard cups containing 8 ounces. Raspberries and cream cheese should be sprinkled on top. Place the remaining bread on top. Whisk the eggs, milk, and syrup together in a small dish, then pour it over the bread. Cover and place in the refrigerator for at least one hour before serving.
2. Bring the temperature of the air fryer to 325 degrees. Put individual servings of custard in individual cups and place them in an air fryer basket. Cook for 12 to 15 minutes, or until the topping is golden brown and puffy.
3. In the meanwhile, whisk together the cornstarch and water in a small saucepan until it is smooth. Add 1-1/2 cups raspberries, lemon juice, syrup, and lemon zest. Bring the water to a boil, then turn the heat down. Cook while stirring for approximately two minutes, or until the mixture has thickened. Remove the seeds and set the liquid aside to gently cool.
4. Mix the remaining half-cup of berries into the syrup in a gentle manner. Cinnamon dust may be added to the French toast cups before serving with maple syrup if preferred.

Scotch Eggs Prepared in an Air Fryer

Preparation time: 10 minutes   Cooking time: 15minutes   Serving: 1

Nutrition

- Calories: 500
- Carbs: 30g
- Protein: 10g
- Fats: 0g

Ingredients

- 1 pound bulk pork sausage
- To taste, salt and pepper are available.
- 6 hard-boiled big eggs
- 1 big egg, beaten using very little force.
- 3/4 of a cup of cornflakes in crushed form

Directions

1. Bring the temperature of the air fryer to 400 degrees. Cut the sausage into six equal pieces, then flatten them and season them with salt and pepper. Mold each part into the shape of a hard-boiled egg that has been peeled. Coat first in beaten egg, then in crumbs made from cornflakes.
2. Put the ingredients in the air fryer basket in a single layer on a greased tray. Cook for 12 to 15 minutes, turning the meat over once halfway through until the center is no longer pink.

Croquettes for breakfast made in the air fryer with eggs and asparagus

Preparation time: 10 minutes **Cooking time: 20minutes** **Serving: 1**

Nutrition:

- Calories: 800
- Carbs: 26g
- Protein: 4g
- Fats: 0g

Ingredients

- 3-and-a-half tablespoons of butter
- 3 tablespoons all-purpose flour
- 3/4 cup 2% milk
- 6 big eggs that have been hard-boiled and then sliced
- 1/2 cup of freshly cut asparagus spears
- half a cup of finely chopped green onions
- 1/3 cup shredded cheddar cheese
- 1 tablespoon of fresh tarragon that has been minced
- 1/4 teaspoon salt
- 1/4 teaspoon pepper
- 1 cup of panko bread crumbs
- 3 big eggs, beaten
- Cooking spray

Directions

1. Butter should be melted in a large pot set over medium heat. After smoothly incorporating the flour, continue to simmer while stirring for an additional one to two minutes. Slowly whisk in the milk, continuing to simmer, and stir until the liquid has thickened (the mixture will be thick). Mix in the eggs that have been hard-boiled, the asparagus, the green onions, the cheese, the tarragon, and the salt and pepper. Put in the refrigerator for at least two hours.
2. Bring the temperature of the air fryer to 350 degrees. Form one-fourth cupful portions of the egg mixture into twelve ovals about three inches in length. Separate the eggs and bread crumbs into two separate basins of similar depth. To coat the logs, first roll them in crumbs, then dip them in egg, and then roll them again in crumbs, patting each time to help the coating stick.
3. Croquettes should be arranged in a single layer and sprayed with cooking spray before being placed in batches within the basket of an air fryer. Cook for 8 to 10 minutes, until the meat, is golden brown. Flip, then spray with cooking spray. Continue cooking for a further 3–5 minutes, until the meat is golden brown.

Air Fryer Breakfast Sweet Potato Skins

Preparation time: 10minutes **Cooking time: 20minutes** **Serving: 2**

Nutrition:

- Calories: 130
- Carbs: 30g
- Protein: 3g
- Fats: 5g

INGREDIENTS

- 2 medium sweet potatoes
- 2 tsp. olive oil
- 4 eggs
- 14 of a cup of whole milk
- salt and pepper
- four fried pieces of bacon
- 2 thinly sliced green onions
- 1 small tomato, chopped

Directions

1. After they have been washed, chop the sweet potatoes into thirds or fourths. To soften them, nuke them in the microwave for six to eight minutes, depending on their size.
2. Cut the potatoes in half lengthwise while protecting your hand with an oven mitt. Remove the flesh of the potato, leaving a margin of 1/4 inch around the edges. You may utilize the sweet potato you scooped out for something else.
3. Olive oil should be brushed over the potato skins, and then salt should be sprinkled on top. Place the skins in the basket of your Air Fryer and set the temperature to 400 degrees Fahrenheit (or the maximum attainable temperature). Cook for ten minutes.
4. In the meanwhile, put the eggs, milk, salt, and pepper in a pan that doesn't stick. Cook the mixture over medium heat, stirring it often, until there are no more liquid eggs visible and the mixture is completely dry.
5. Place one piece of crumbled bacon and one-quarter of the scrambled eggs in the center of each potato skin that has been cooked. Spread the crumbled cheese over top. Place back into the basket of the air fryer and continue cooking at 400 degrees for another three minutes, or until the cheese has melted.
6. To serve, top each portion with tomato and green onion.

Cookies Prepared with an Air Fryer

Preparation time: 10 minutes **Cooking time: 15 minutes** **Serving: 1 to 2**

Nutrition:

- Calories: 330
- Carbs: 42.5g
- Protein: 4.0g
- Fats: 1.9g

Ingredients

- 1 cup of ripe bananas that have been mashed (about 2 medium)
- 1/2 cup of peanut butter with chunks.
- Honey, measured in cups, and vanilla essence, in teaspoons.
- 1 cup of traditional rolled oats
- 1/2 cup of flour made from whole wheat
- a quarter cup of low-fat powdered milk
- 2 teaspoons of cinnamon in ground form
- 1/2 teaspoon salt
- 1/4 teaspoon baking soda
- 1 cup of dried cranberries or raisins, whatever you choose.

Directions

1. Bring the temperature of the air fryer to 300 degrees. Bananas, peanut butter, honey, and vanilla extract should be mixed until smooth. In a separate bowl, whisk together the oats, flour, milk powder, cinnamon, salt, and baking soda. Then, gradually beat this mixture into the banana mixture. Cranberries, dried, should be stirred in.
2. Place the tray in the air fryer and grease it. Working in batches, drop the dough by 1/4 cupful onto the tray and spread it out to a thickness of 1/2 inch.
3. Cook for 6 to 8 minutes, until it has a very light brown color. Cool in the basket for 1 minute. Transfer to cooling racks with wire.
4. Prepare and serve either hot or at room temperature.

Candied Bacon Finished In the Air Fryer

Preparation time: 15 minutes **Cooking time: 20 minutes** **Serving: 2**

Nutrition:

- Calories: 178
- Carbs: 45g
- Protein: 1g
- Fats: 1g

Ingredients

- 1 teaspoon of butter
- 1/4 tsp. of miso paste in white
- Honey or maple syrup to taste, six teaspoons
- 1 tablespoon of vinegar made from rice
- 8 ounces of bacon with a thick cut.

Instructions

Heat the air fryer to 390 degrees Fahrenheit.

1. Butter should be melted over medium heat in a saucepan of appropriate size. After that, raise the temperature to medium-high and add the honey, rice wine vinegar, and miso paste to the pan. Stir the mixture until all of the ingredients are completely incorporated, then bring it to a boil. Take it away from the heat and put it to the side.
2. Fry the bacon in the air fryer for three to four minutes on each side after placing it in a single layer (make sure it doesn't overlap!) Apply a very thin coating of the miso glaze to one side of the bacon using a pastry brush, and then continue to air fry the bacon for an additional minute. When it is done, it should have a crisp outside and a sticky inside.

Cheesy Breakfast Egg Rolls

Preparation time: 10 minutes **Cooking time: 20 minutes Serving: 2**

Nutrition:

- Calories: 209
- Carbs: 19g
- Protein: 10g
- Fats: 10g

Ingredients

- 1/2-pound bulk pork sausage
- a quarter of a cup of shredded extra-sharp cheddar cheese
- Monterey Jack cheese, shredded, equal to a half cup
- 1 tablespoon of green onions that have been chopped
- 4 big eggs
- 1 tablespoon 2% milk
- 1/4 teaspoon salt
- 1/8 teaspoon pepper
- 1 tablespoon butter
- 12 wonton wrappers for egg rolls
- Cooking spray
- Optional: Maple syrup or salsa

Directions

1. Cook the sausage over medium heat in a small nonstick pan until it is no longer pink, about 4-6 minutes, breaking it up into crumbles as it cooks; then drain. Mix in the cheeses, then put aside the green onions. Wipe skillet clean.
2. Whisk the eggs, milk, salt, and pepper together in a small bowl until everything is combined. Melt some butter in the same pan you've been using over medium heat. Pour in the egg mixture, then continue to heat and stir it until the eggs have become thick and there is no liquid egg left. Stir in sausage mixture.
3. Bring the temperature of the air fryer to 400 degrees. Place a quarter cup of the filling slightly below the center of an egg roll wrapper, with one of the corners of the wrapper facing you. (Until you are ready to use the wrappers, cover any that are left over with a moist paper towel.) Fold the bottom corner over the filling, then use water to wet the wrapper edges that remain. Over the filling, fold the side corners toward the center. The egg roll should be rolled up firmly and then pressed to seal at the tip. Repeat.
4. Egg rolls should be arranged in a single layer and sprayed with cooking spray before being placed in the air fryer basket. This should be done in batches. Cook for three to four minutes, until it has a very light brown color. Flip, then spray with cooking spray. Continue cooking for a further 3–4 minutes, until the bacon is crisp and golden brown. If you choose, you may serve this dish with maple syrup or salsa on the side.

The Banana Bread Pizza Made In the Air Fryer

Preparation time: 15 minutes **Cooking time: 25minutes** **Serving: 2**

Nutrition:

- Calories: 410
- Carbs: 4g
- Protein: 29g
- Fats: 162g

Ingredients

- 3 ripe bananas mashed
- 1 1/2 tsp baking powder
- 1/4 tsp baking soda
- 1 tablespoon of cinnamon
- 1 egg
- 1 ounce of dark brown sugar
- 3 1/2 cups flour
- 1 ounce of powdered sugar for rolling the dough.
- A Layer of Cream Cheese
- 1 ounce and eight ounces of cream cheese, softened
- 2/3 cup sugar
- Toppings
- 1 21 oz can apple pie filling
- 1/2 cup pecans caramel syrup for drizzling

Instructions

1. Bananas that have reached their peak ripeness, baking soda, baking powder, eggs, cinnamon, and brown sugar should be combined in a mixing dish. Combine everything.
2. Mix in some flour with the ingredients. Mix well until a robust dough is produced.
3. Cut the dough in half horizontally. Form a ball out of each half of the dough, then roll the balls in powdered sugar to keep them from sticking to the counter.
4. Make sure each ball can fit into the basket of the air fryer by flattening it into a round disc.
5. Cooking spray should be applied to two square pieces of parchment paper, and then one disc of dough should be placed on each piece. Make sure the disc of the dough is at least two inches larger than the piece of parchment paper you're using.

Topping made with cream cheese

1. Put the cream cheese that has been softened and the sugar in a little bowl. Combine everything by stirring it until there are no more lumps.
2. On top of the dough discs for the banana bread, spread the cream cheese mixture.
3. Spread one-half of the apple filling over the top of each pizza. If you so choose, add some pecans.

Instructions for an Air Fryer

1. Start by preheating the Air Fryer at 350 degrees for at least three minutes.

2. When you are ready to make the first pizza, insert parchment paper in the air fryer basket in a meticulous manner. Pizza made using banana bread should be cooked for 15 minutes. Grab the ends of the parchment paper and remove the pizza from the baking sheet.
3. Please allow it to cool. Wait 15 minutes before serving the second pizza.
4. Caramel syrup should be drizzled over the Banana Bread Pizza after it has been placed on big plates.

Air-Fried Ham and Egg Pockets in the Air Fryer

Preparation time: 8 to 9 minutes **Cooking time: 15minutes** **Serving: 2**

Nutrition:

- Calories: 180
- Carbs: 6g
- Protein: 20g
- Fats: 7g

Ingredients

- 1 big egg
- 2 teaspoons 2% milk
- 2 grams of butter, melted
- 1 ounce of deli ham that has been cut very thinly and chopped
- 2 teaspoons of shredded aged cheddar
- 1 tube of refrigerator crescent rolls (four ounces total)

Directions

1. Bring the temperature of the air fryer to 300 degrees. Eggs and milk should be mixed in a small bowl. In a small skillet, heat butter until hot. After adding the egg mixture, continue to cook the dish while stirring it over medium heat until the eggs are fully set. Take the dish away from the heat. Ham and cheese should be folded in.
2. Cut the crescent roll dough into two separate rectangles. After the holes have been sealed, divide the filling in half and spoon half of it down the middle of each rectangle. Fold the excess dough over the filling and crimp the edges to seal. Put the ingredients in the air fryer basket in a single layer on a greased tray. Cook for 8 to 10 minutes, until the meat, is golden brown.

Mini Nutella Doughnut Holes Made with an Air Fryer

Preparation time: 10 minutes **Cooking time: 15 minutes** **Serving: 2**

Nutrition:

- Calories: 100
- Carbs: 16g
- Protein: 20g
- Fats: 4g

Ingredients

- 1 big egg
- 1 teaspoon of water in total
- 1 tube of big flaky biscuits from the refrigerator, 16.3 ounces total (8 counts)
- 2/3 cup Nutella

Directions

1. Bring the temperature of the air fryer to 300 degrees. Mix the water and the egg. On a surface dusted with flour, flatten out each biscuit into a circle of 6 inches in diameter.
2. Next, cut each circle into four equal wedges. Lightly coat each wedge with the egg mixture, then finish with one teaspoon of Nutella on top. Pull the corners up over the filling, then squeeze the sides together tightly to seal.
3. Place the wedges in the air fryer basket one at a time in a single layer on a tray that has not been oiled. Cook for 8 to 10 minutes, turning once until the meat is golden brown. Sugar powder may be used, and the dessert should be served warm.

Bourbon bacon cooked in an air fryer

Preparation time: 10minutes**Cooking time: 15minutes****Serving: 2**

Nutrition:

- Calories: 180
- Carbs: 27g
- Protein: 19g
- Fats: 7g

Ingredients

- 8 rashers of bacon
- 34 of a cup of bourbon
- 1 tube (12.4 ounces) of cinnamon buns that have been chilled and come with icing
- 12 cups of pecans that have been chopped
- 2 tablespoons maple syrup
- 1 milligram of fresh gingerroot that has been minced

Directions

1. Put the bacon in a shallow dish, and then pour the bourbon over it. Refrigerate overnight after sealing the container. Take out the bacon and blot it dry, then throw away the bourbon.
2. Cook the bacon in many batches in a large pan over medium heat until it is almost completely crisp but still flexible. Remove to paper towels so the excess liquid may drain. Throw away all of the drippings except for one teaspoon.
3. Bring the temperature of the air fryer to 350 degrees. Cut the dough into eight individual rolls, storing the frosting package for later use. Unroll spiral rolls into long strips, then press dough to make strips that are 6 inches long and 1 inch wide. Place one piece of bacon on each strip of dough, cutting the bacon to fit as necessary, then reroll the dough into a spiral shape. To create a seal, pinch the ends. Repeat with the remaining portion of the dough. Put four rolls on a tray that has not been oiled and put it in the air fryer basket. Cook for five minutes. After about 4 minutes, flip the rolls over and continue cooking until they are golden brown.
4. In the meanwhile, mix the maple syrup and pecans together. In a separate dish, combine the ginger with the contents of the icing package, and whisk. The leftover bacon drippings should be heated over a medium flame in the same skillet. Add the pecan mixture, and continue cooking for another 2 to 3 minutes while tossing it regularly until it is gently browned.
5. Warm cinnamon buns should have half of the frosting drizzled over them, and then half of the nuts sprinkled on top. To produce a second batch, just repeat the process.

Sticks of French toast cooked in an air fryer

Preparation time: 35 minutes **Cooking time: 1 hour** **Serving: 2**

Nutrition:

- Calories: 150
- Carbs: 31g
- Protein: 19g
- Fats: 10g

Ingredients

- 6 old pieces of Texas toast from the previous day
- 4 big eggs
- 1 cup 2% milk
- 2 tablespoons sugar
- 1 teaspoon vanilla extract
- a quarter to half of a teaspoon of cinnamon powder
- 1 cup of crushed cornflakes, with the possibility of using more
- Sugar for confections, on your initiative
- Maple syrup

Directions

1. Each slice of bread should be cut into thirds, then placed in a 13-by-9-inch dish that has not been oiled. Eggs, milk, sugar, vanilla, and cinnamon are mixed together in a large dish using a whisk. Spread it over the bread and soak it for two minutes, turning it over once. If you so choose, you may cover both sides of the bread with cornflake crumbs.
2. Place in a baking dish that is 15 by 10 by 1 inch and has been oiled. Freeze until hard, approximately 45 minutes. Transfer to a freezer-safe container with a tight-fitting lid, and then store in the freezer.
3. To prepare frozen French toast sticks, do the following: Bring the temperature of the air fryer to 350 degrees. Put the necessary quantity onto a greased tray and place it in the air fryer basket. Prepare for three minutes. Cook for a further 2–3 minutes, turning once until the bottom is golden brown. Depending on your preferences, dust with confectioner's sugar. Prepare with syrup and serve.

Air-Fryer Red Potatoes

Preparation time: 10 minutes   **Cooking time: 20 minutes**   **Serving: 2**

Nutrition:

- Calories: 100
- Carbs: 34g
- Protein: 16g
- Fats: 12g

Ingredients

- 2 kg of tiny red potatoes left unpeeled and sliced into wedges.
- 2 tablespoons olive oil
- 1 tablespoon of fresh rosemary that has been chopped, or 1 teaspoon of dried rosemary that has been crushed
- 2 cloves of garlic, finely chopped
- 1/2 teaspoon salt
- 1/4 teaspoon pepper

Directions

1. Bring the temperature of the air fryer to 400 degrees. Oil should be drizzled over the potatoes. The rosemary, garlic, salt, and pepper should be sprinkled on top, then the mixture should be gently tossed to coat.
2. Place the air fryer basket on a tray that has not been oiled. 10 to 12 minutes total cooking time, with one toss while cooking, until potatoes are golden brown and soft.

Puff Pastry Danishes Baked in an Air Fryer

Preparation time: 10 minutes **Cooking time: 15 minutes** **Serving: 2**

Nutrition:

- Calories: 140
- Carbs: 18g
- Protein: 21g
- Fats: 10g

Ingredients

- 1 container of cream cheese (eight ounces), softened to room temperature
- 1/4 cup sugar
- 2 tablespoons all-purpose flour
- 1/2 teaspoon vanilla extract
- 2 big egg yolks
- 1 teaspoon of water in total
- 1 packet of frozen puff pastry, 17.3 ounces total weight, defrosted
- 1/3 cup seedless raspberry jam or your preferred flavor of seedless jam

Directions

1. Bring the temperature of the air fryer to 325 degrees. Cream cheese, sugar, flour, and vanilla extract should be mixed together until smooth before adding one egg yolk.
2. Combine the remaining egg yolk with the water. Unfold each sheet of puff pastry and roll it out into a square of 12 inches on a surface that has been gently dusted with flour. Divide each into nine squares measuring 4 inches.
3. Spread one spoonful of the cream cheese mixture and one rounded teaspoon of jam on top of each square. Bring two corners of the pastry that are opposite one another over the filling, and seal with the egg yolk mixture. Coat the tops with the remaining egg yolk mixture and brush.
4. Place the food in the air fryer basket in single layers, one at a time, using oiled trays. Cook for 8 to 10 minutes, until the meat, is golden brown. To be served hot. Refrigerate leftovers.

Lunch Recipes

The Ultimate Spinach and Artichoke Dip

Preparation time: 10 minutes **Cooking time:** 15 minutes **Serving:** 2

Nutrition:

- Calories: 250
- Carbs: 20g
- Protein: 19g
- Fats: 5g

Ingredients

- 3 tbsp. butter
- 4 tablespoons of minced garlic
- 1 bag spinach
- Various amounts of salt & pepper, to taste
- 2 cans of artichoke hearts, which have been drained and washed.
- 3 tbsp. butter (additional)
- 3 tablespoons of flour
- 1 and a half cups of whole milk (more if needed)
- 1 package (8 ounces) of cream cheese that has been softened
- 1/2 tablespoon of crumbled feta
- 12 cups of grated parmesan cheese
- 3/4 of a cup of grated Pepper Jack cheese
- 1/4 of a teaspoon of cayenne
- Additional grated Pepper Jack cheese
- Crackers, pita wedges, and tortilla chips all make an appearance.

Directions

1. Melt 3 tablespoons butter in a pan over medium heat. After a couple of minutes, add the garlic that has been minced and continue to simmer. Raise the temperature slightly, then add the spinach to the pan. As the spinach begins to wilt, stir it about and continue to simmer for a couple more minutes. Take the spinach out of the pan and place it in a fine mesh strainer. Squeeze any more juice that has collected into the pan. Put the spinach to the side for now.
2. Put the artichokes in the pan and cook them for a few minutes over medium-high heat, stirring occasionally, until the liquid has evaporated and the artichokes have developed a little bit of color. Take the artichokes out of the dish.
3. To produce a paste, melt three more tablespoons of butter in the same pan or a separate pot, and then whisk in three more tablespoons of flour until the mixture is smooth. After cooking for a minute or two at a heat setting somewhere between medium and low, pour in the milk. Continue to stir while cooking until the mixture begins to slightly thicken; if necessary, add a splash more milk.
4. Stir continuously after the addition of the cream cheese, feta, Parmesan, pepper jack, and cayenne until all of the cheese has melted and the sauce is smooth. Prepare the artichokes and spinach by chopping them, then add them to the sauce. Stir to mix.

5. Pour into a baking dish that has been greased. Bake at 375 degrees for 15 minutes, or until the cheese is melted and bubbling, then top with more shredded pepper jack and bake.
6. Serve with slices of pita bread, potato chips, or crackers!

Caviar

Preparation time: 10 minutes **Cooking time: 20 minutes** **Serving: 2**

Nutrition:

- Calories: 200
- Carbs: 11g
- Protein: 15g
- Fats: 6g

Ingredients

- One can of black-eyed peas, drained and washed after being drained.
- 1 can of black beans, 15 ounces, drained and washed before using
- 1 1/2 c. diced roma tomatoes
- 1 chopped jalapeno pepper, 1 chopped yellow bell pepper, 1/2 cup chopped red onion, 1/4 cup chopped cilantro
- Three tablespoons of olive oil
- 2 tablespoons of vinegar made from red wine
- Worcestershire sauce, one tablespoon
- half of a teaspoon of seasoned salt
- 1/2 milligrams of ground cumin
- 1/2 milligrams of black pepper, ground
- Chips made of tortilla, for serving

Directions

1. Use a large mixing bowl to combine the black-eyed peas, black beans, tomato, bell pepper, red onion, jalapeno, cilantro, olive oil, vinegar, Worcestershire sauce, seasoned salt, cumin, and black pepper.
2. Combine everything by thoroughly combining it. To be served in conjunction with tortilla chips.

Broccoli cheese soup

Preparation time: 10 minutes   **Cooking time : 15 minutes**   **Serving: 1**

Nutrition:

- Calories:587
- Carbs: 25g
- Protein: 25g
- Fats: 6g

Ingredients

- 1 full onion chopped and set aside.
- 1 stick butter
- 1/3 c. flour
- 4 ounces of full-fat milk
- 2 tablespoons of half-and-half
- 4 broccoli crowns, each of which is separated into florets
- 1 milligram of nutmeg
- 3 tablespoons of grated cheese (mild cheddar, sharp cheddar, jack, etc.)
- Add just a pinch of salt (more if needed)
- Black pepper that has been freshly ground.
- 2 cups of chicken broth, to be used for thinning if necessary.

Directions

1. In a saucepan, melt the butter over medium heat, then add the onions to the pot. After the onions have been cooking for three to four minutes, flour should be distributed over the surface of the onions. After giving everything a good stir to incorporate, you should let it simmer for about a minute before adding the milk and the half-and-half. Nutmeg should be added first, followed by broccoli, a pinch of salt, and a generous amount of black pepper.
2. Cover and bring the heat down to a low setting. Maintain a low simmer for twenty to thirty minutes, or until the broccoli is cooked through. Mix in the cheese, then waits for it to melt.
3. Try the seasonings and make any necessary adjustments. The dish may then be served as is, mashed using a potato masher to slightly reduce the size of the broccoli pieces, or transferred to a blender in two separate batches and pureed. (If you purée it in a blender, bring it back to the fire and let it become hot for a while. If more liquid is required to thin the sauce, add a splash of chicken broth. Enjoy!

Homemade Chicken Apple Sausage

Preparation time: 10 minutes   **Cooking time: 20 minutes**   **Serving: 2**

Nutrition:

- Calories: 140
- Carbs: 25g
- Protein: 14g
- Fats: 6g

Ingredients

- 1 apple Granny Smith, unpeeled and cored
- 1.05 kg of ground chicken
- 2 cloves of garlic, micro-planed to a fine powder.
- 2 chopped scallions in total
- 1 tsp. kosher salt
- 1/2 tsp. black pepper
- 1/2 tsp. fennel seeds
- a quarter of a teaspoon of crushed red pepper
- A little bit of nutmeg
- 4 tsp. vegetable oil, divided

Directions

1. Using a box grater with big holes, shred the apple directly onto a cutting board. Discard the apple's core as well as the stem. The grated apple should be placed inside a paper towel, and the liquid should be gently wrung out while you hold on to the apple itself. After it has been granted, the apple should be roughly chopped and placed in a big basin.
2. Put the chopped apple in a bowl and add the ground chicken, garlic, scallions, salt, pepper, fennel seeds, and crushed red pepper to it. Nutmeg should also be added. Make sure to use your hands to thoroughly incorporate all of the sausage ingredients. Form into eight balls, then put on a baking sheet lined with parchment paper.
3. In a big pan made of cast iron, bring to a medium-low temperature 2 tablespoons of the oil. Create four patties with a width of three inches each and set them in the pan that has been warmed. Cook the sausage patties for six to eight minutes, or until browned on both sides and cooked all the way through. Place the chicken on a platter, then cover it with foil to keep it warm. Repeat the process with the remaining sausage patties and oil. To be served hot.

The Very Best Cinnamon Rolls

Preparation time: 15 minutes **Cooking time: 20 minutes** **Serving: 2**

Nutrition:

- Calories: 250
- Carbs: 20g
- Protein: 19g
- Fats: 5g

Ingredients

- 1 fluid ounce of whole milk
- 1 c. Vegetable oil
- 1 c. Sugar
- 2 active dry yeast packages (packages) (0.25-ounce packets)
- 8 c. (plus 1 cup extra, reserved) (plus 1 cup extra, reserved) flour suited for all purposes
- 1 tsp. (heaping) baking powder
- 1 tsp. (scant) baking soda
- 1 tbsp. (heaping) salt
- Lots of butter has been melted.
- 2 c. Sugar
- Dusting of cinnamon

FOR THE FROSTING MADE OF MAPLE

- 1 bag powdered sugar
- 2 tsp. maple flavoring
- 1/2 c. milk
- 1/4 c. melted butter
- 1/4 c. brewed coffee
- 1/8 tsp. salt

Directions

1. To prepare the dough: In a medium saucepan set over medium heat, bring the milk, vegetable oil, and sugar to a temperature that is almost as high as a boil. Put to the side and let warm up. After sprinkling the yeast on top, let it rest for a minute while it absorbs the milk.
2. Mix in a total of 8 cups of flour. After stirring until the ingredients are almost completely blended, cover with a clean dish towel and put away in an area that is generally warm for an hour. After an hour, take the cloth off the bowl and add the baking powder, baking soda, salt, and the last cup of flour to the mixture. To incorporate everything, give it a good stir. You may use the dough right immediately, or you can put it in a mixing basin and refrigerate it for up to three days. If the dough rises to the top of the bowl, punch it down and continue using the bowl. (It's important to note that the dough will be much simpler to deal with if you refrigerate it for at least an hour or two before you begin.)

3. Take half of the dough out of the pan or basin and set it aside. Next, construct the rolls. On a baking surface dusted with flour, lay out the dough into a big rectangle measuring about 30 by 10 inches. Roll out the dough to an extremely thin thickness.

4. Pour between three-quarters and one full cup of melted butter over the top of the dough to begin making the filling. Make an even application of the butter by spreading it out with your fingertips. On top of the butter, generously sprinkle one-half of the ground cinnamon and one cup of the sugar. You shouldn't be scared to add extra sugar or butter after you finish the dish. The idea is for it to be gooey.

5. Start rolling the rectangle firmly towards you by starting at the end that is the furthest away from you. Employ both hands, move gently, and be mindful to maintain the roll as compact as possible. Don't be alarmed if some of the fillings leak out as you're working on the rolls; this just indicates that they're going to be delicious. When you come to the end, you need to squeeze the seam together and then turn the roll over so that the seam is facing the other direction. When you are done, you will have one long log that is gooey, buttery, cinnamony, and sweet.

6. Place a cutting board below the roll, and using a sharp knife, cut the roll into pieces that are half an inch thick. 20–25 rolls may be produced from a single wood. Spread a couple of tablespoons' worth of melted butter in the bottom of disposable foil cake pans (or conventional round cake pans measuring 9 inches in diameter) and swirl to coat. Put the cut rolls into the pans, but make sure they aren't crammed in too tightly. (There is enough for seven to nine rolls in each pan.)

7. Roll out the remaining half of the dough and repeat the sugar and butter coating procedure with the other pans. Turn the temperature in the oven up to 375 degrees. Before beginning the baking process, make sure each of the pans is covered with a dish towel and left on the countertop to rise for at least 20 minutes. Take off the cloth, and continue baking for another 15 to 18 minutes, or until the topping is golden brown. It is important to prevent the rolls from being too browned.

8. Prepare the maple frosting while the buns are in the oven by following these steps: Combine the powdered sugar, milk, butter, coffee, and salt in a large bowl and mix together until smooth. Add a few drops of the maple flavor. Whisk until the consistency is fairly smooth. Test the consistency of the icing and, if necessary, add more maple, sugar, butter, or any of the other components until it is of the desired consistency. The consistency of the frosting needs to be relatively thick while yet being quite pourable.

9. Take the pans out of the oven and set them aside. As soon as possible, sprinkle icing all over the top. Be careful to get it to the top and around the edges. As time passes, the rolls will be able to take on some of the taste and moisture of the icing. They don't improve with age... not that they're around for more than a few seconds at a time, either. Make some today and give them to a friend! It will solidify our connection for the rest of our lives. I promise.

Chickpea Tot Hot dish

Preparation time: 20minutes   Cooking time: 40 mint   Serving: 2

Nutrition:

- Calories: 180
- Carbs: 27g
- Protein: 19g
- Fats: 7g

Ingredients

- 6 tablespoons of unfiltered extra virgin olive oil
- 1 yellow onion, medium-sized, cut very finely
- 2 big carrots, peeled, cored, and cut very finely
- 2 substantial celery stalks, cut very coarsely
- Kosher salt
- 4 cloves of garlic, cut very coarsely
- 2 tsp. Aleppo pepper or smoked paprika
- Black pepper that has been freshly ground.
- 1 tbsp. harissa paste or dried harissa
- 1 tbsp. tomato paste
- 1/2 tablespoon of dry white wine
- 2 cans of chickpeas, each containing 15 ounces, drained and rinsed
- 1 chopped tomato can weigh 28 ounces
- half a cup of water
- 1 tsp. sugar
- 2 pounds. frozen tater tots
- A couple of squeezes of lemon juice
- The topping ingredients consist of chopped cilantro and flat-leaf parsley.
- Crumbled feta as a topping, which is optional.
- A dollop of plain Greek yogurt on the side to serve, although this is optional.

Directions

1. Place a rack in the top third of the oven and heat the oven to 450 degrees Fahrenheit while you do this.
2. Place the olive oil in a large Dutch oven, braiser, or skillet and bring it to medium-high heat. The pan should be able to withstand oven use and should have a capacity of at least 3.5 quarts. When the oil is heated, add the onion, carrots, and celery along with a bit of salt. Cook for 10 to 15 minutes while tossing the vegetables regularly until they become mushy.
3. After one minute has passed, add the garlic, Aleppo pepper or paprika, and a few turns of black pepper, and continue to cook while stirring.
4. Add the harissa, tomato paste, and white wine to the pan and cook over medium heat, stirring occasionally, for three to four minutes, or until the wine has been reduced by half.

5. Add the chickpeas, tomatoes, water, sugar, and two generous pinches of salt, and stir all of the ingredients together. Raise the temperature so that the mixture comes to a boil. Bring to a simmer, then cover and continue cooking for another 15 minutes, stirring the mixture regularly. Try it out, then make any necessary adjustments to the seasoning.
6. If the pan you are using cannot be placed in the oven, transfer the contents of the skillet to a casserole dish measuring 13 by 9 inches (or something of a similar size); if the skillet can be placed in the oven, keep the mixture in the skillet. Spread a layer of the tots on top. Add little salt and pepper before serving. Bake the tots until they have a golden color; start checking them at the 35-minute mark to see if they are done.
7. If using, sprinkle the top with a few squeezes of lemon juice, herbs, and feta, and serve with dollops of Greek yogurt on the side, if preferred.

Quick BBQ Sausage Sloppy Joes

Preparation time: 10 minutes **Cooking time: 15 minutes** **Servings: 1**

Nutrition:

- Calories: 140
- Carbs: 25g
- Protein: 14g
- Fats: 6g

Ingredients

- 1 package of Original Sausage Crumbles in the original flavor
- 1 c. barbecue sauce
- 1 can tomato sauce
- 8 hamburger buns or kaiser rolls
- 1 c. shredded sharp Cheddar cheese

Directions

1. Place the sausage, tomato sauce, and barbecue sauce into a medium-sized pot and mix well. Cook for eight to ten minutes over medium heat, stirring regularly, or until the food reaches the desired temperature.
2. The second step is to stuff the buns with the sausage mixture and the cheese.

Crepes that Have Been Folded, Filled with Smoked Ham, and Topped with Butter

Preparation time: 10 minutes   **Cooking time: 15 minutes**   **Serving: 1**

Nutrition:

- Calories: 130
- Carbs: 30g
- Protein: 3g
- Fats: 5g

Ingredients

- Salted butter
- Basic crêpes
- Smoked ham with freshly ground black pepper

Directions

1. First, spread some salted butter on a crêpe, ideally made with buckwheat flour. Pepper that has been freshly ground should be sprinkled on top.
2. Place a thin slice of smoked ham on top of the dish. Crêpes should be folded in half, then again in half. Iterate the process to produce more crepes. Immediately serve after cooking.

Open "Face" Egg Salad Sandwiches

Preparation time: 10 minutes **Cooking time: 15 minutes** **Serving: 1**

Nutrition:

- Calories: 100
- Carbs: 25g
- Protein: 25g
- Fats: 3g

Ingredients

- 7 eggs
- 1/4 c. mayonnaise
- 2 tsp. mustard
- 1/2 tsp. salt 1/2 tsp. ground pepper
- 1 thin piece of ham

Directions

1. Pour enough water into a medium saucepan to cover the eggs. Bring to a boil, then continue cooking for another 2 minutes with the lid off. After removing it from the heat, cover it and let it stand for ten minutes. Put the eggs in a dish and run cold water over them until they are cool. Peel eggs.
2. Use an egg slicer or a knife to cut two eggs into thin slices. Put eight of the slices to the side for the eyes. Put the leftover pieces in a basin and add the eggs that have not been cut. Combine using a fork to mash. Mix in the mayonnaise, mustard, salt, and ground pepper by stirring everything together.
3. Spread a thin layer of mayonnaise on each of the four pieces of bread, and then top each slice with either egg salad or a slice of ham. Create expressions of your choosing with egg slices, egg salad, and the toppings listed below. Immediately serve after cooking.

Pimiento Grilled Cheese

Preparation time: 15 minutes   **Cooking time: 25 minutes**   **Serving: 2**

Nutrition:

- Calories: 400
- Carbs: 20g
- Protein: 19g
- Fats: 7g

Ingredients

- 8 oz. Sharp cheddar cheese
- 3/4 c. Low-fat mayonnaise
- 1 red bell pepper that has been roasted
- 3/4 tsp. Apple cider vinegar
- 3/4 tsp. Sriracha chili sauce
- 1/4 milligrams of dried garlic
- 1/4 milligram of onion powder
- 1/4 tsp. Salt
- A quarter of a milligram of freshly ground black pepper one milligram of cayenne pepper
- 8 thick slices of quality white bread (like Pullman)
- 4 tbsp. Unsalted butter

Directions

1. First, in a large bowl, thoroughly combine all the ingredients, except for the bread and the butter. Refrigerate for 2 hours to allow flavors to combine. (This recipe yields around 2 cups. The shelf life of pimiento cheese in the refrigerator is about one week. Before usage, make sure the temperature is at room temperature.
2. Smear each of the four pieces of bread with a quarter of a cup of pimiento cheese. Place the second piece of bread on top of each one. One side of each sandwich should have 1 1/2 teaspoons of butter spread on it.
3. Bring a big pan that doesn't cling to the food to medium-low heat. Put two sandwiches in the pan with the buttered side facing down. Cook for three to four minutes, or until the bread is golden brown. Spread one and a half teaspoons of butter on the opposite side of each sandwich before placing it in the oven to cook the first side. Flip the sandwiches and continue cooking for an additional three to four minutes, until the second side is crispy and golden brown, and the cheese has melted. Proceed in the same manner with the remaining two sandwiches.

Kid-Friendly Pizzadillas

Preparation time: 15 minutes   **Cooking time: 25 minutes**   **Serving: 2**

Nutrition:

- Calories: 210
- Carbs: 29g
- Protein: 19g
- Fats: 4g

Ingredients

- 1 tbsp. canola oil
- 4 flour tortillas made without fat
- 1 1/2 c. shredded part-skim mozzarella cheese
- 1 oz. turkey pepperoni
- 1 c. marinara sauce

Directions

1. Set the oven temperature to 400 degrees Fahrenheit.
2. Coat a jellyroll pan with canola oil using a brush, then place tortillas on top. On top of each tortilla, sprinkle three tablespoons of grated cheese, and then divide the pepperoni among the tortillas. Put three tablespoons of cheese on top of each one. Bake at 400 degrees F for 5 minutes.
3. After removing it from the oven, fold each tortilla in half with extreme care. Continue baking for a further 10 minutes, flipping once after the first 5 minutes, or until the food is golden and crisp. To accompany the marinara, serve.

Salad made with creamy chicken

Preparation time: 10 minutes   **Cooking time:** 15 minutes   **Serving:** 1

Nutrition:

- Calories: 150
- Carbs: 26g
- Protein: 25g
- Fats: 9g

Ingredients

- Chicken breast halves skinless and boneless weighing 2 pounds
- 1/2 c. light mayonnaise
- 1/2 tablespoon of plain, nonfat Greek yogurt
- 1 tbsp. fresh lemon juice
- 1 tablespoon of vinegar made from white wine
- 1 tbsp. Dijon mustard
- 1 milligram of honey
- 1/2 tsp. kosher salt
- 1/2 milligrams of freshly ground black pepper 1 cup of chopped celery 1 cup of dried cranberries that have been sweetened
- 7 tablespoons of smoked almonds that have been roughly chopped

Directions

1. Bring water to a boil in a Dutch oven that has been filled two-thirds of the way.
2. Cover each side of a chicken breast in a single layer of heavy-duty plastic wrap and roll it up securely. Put the chicken into the water that is already boiling. Simmer, covered, for twenty minutes, or until a thermometer reaches 165 degrees Fahrenheit, whichever comes first. Take out of the pan, and let it stand for five minutes. Unwrap the chicken and shred it, then place it in the refrigerator for at least half an hour or until it is cold.
3. Mayonnaise and the following seven ingredients (through black pepper) should be mixed together in a large bowl using a whisk until everything is evenly distributed. Toss the chicken with the remaining 1/3 cup of celery, the cranberries, and the almonds after adding the chicken. Cover and chill for 1 hour. Serve over salad greens.

Hawaiian Plate Lunch with Macaroni Salad

Preparation time: 15 minutes **Cooking time: 25 minutes** **Serving: 2**

Nutrition:

- Calories: 190
- Carbs: 4g
- Protein: 25g
- Fats: 19g

Ingredients

- Potatoes, either red or Yukon Gold, 1 pound
- 1 packet of elbow macaroni
- 1 ½ tbs. mayonnaise
- Three ribs of celery
- 2 prepared by peeling and grating
- 2 hard-boiled eggs
- 12 pounds of ham and 12 cups of frozen peas
- pickled dill cucumbers, chopped, one-half cup
- 1/4 of a cup of red onion that has been coarsely chopped
- 2 milligrams of seasoned salt
- 1/2 tsp. Black pepper that has been freshly ground.

Directions

1. First, bring to a boil two very big saucepans filled with salted water.
2. Cube the potatoes into pieces measuring 1 inch each. They should be cooked in one saucepan of boiling water for approximately eight minutes, or until they can be easily pierced with a fork. Drain well and then put it to the side.
3. Cook the elbow macaroni in the second pot of boiling water until it reaches the "al dente" stage, following the instructions that are printed on the box. After a thorough draining, put it aside.
4. The fourth step is to place the potatoes and noodles in a big salad dish. Toss the mixture once you've added the last of the ingredients. If desired, add a little extra seasoned salt and ground black pepper. Cover and store the salad in the refrigerator until it is time to serve.

Air Fryer Broccoli

Preparation time: 10 minutes **Cooking time: 15 minutes** **Serving: 1**

Nutrition:

- Calories: 160
- Carbs: 24g
- Protein: 25g
- Fats: 9g

Ingredients

- 1 medium-sized broccoli head, broken down into florets
- 1 garlic clove, finely chopped
- 1 tbsp. extra-virgin olive oil
- Kosher salt
- Black pepper that has been freshly ground.
- A few crushed red pepper flakes in a pinch.

Directions

1. Place the broccoli in a large bowl and mix it with the garlic, oil, and black pepper. Season it with salt, black pepper, and red pepper flakes.
2. Arrange the broccoli in a single layer in the basket of an air fryer, working in batches if required. Cook for about 10 minutes at 370 degrees until soft and crispy.

Air Fryer Brussels sprouts

Preparation time: 15 minutes **Cooking time: 25 minutes** **Serving: 2**

Nutrition:

- Calories: 400
- Carbs: 20g
- Protein: 19g
- Fats: 7g

Ingredients

- 1 pound of Brussels sprouts, cleaned and cut in half lengthwise
- 1 tbsp. extra-virgin olive oil
- Kosher salt
- Black pepper that has been freshly ground.
- A few crushed red pepper flakes in a pinch.
- Juice from one-half of a lemon
- 1 garlic clove, finely chopped
- 1 tablespoon of honey
- 1 tablespoon of vinegar made from red wine
- 2 tsp. Dijon mustard

Directions

1. Place the Brussels sprouts in a medium basin and mix them with the oil. Season them with salt, black pepper, and red pepper flakes, then toss them once more.
2. Arrange the sprouts in a single layer into the basket of the air fryer, working in batches if required; set aside the bowl. Cook at 380 degrees for approximately 18 minutes, turning once halfway through, until browned all over and burned in some parts.
3. Combine the lemon juice, garlic, honey, vinegar, and mustard in a small bowl and whisk until smooth. Season with salt and black pepper.
4. Place the cooked Brussels sprouts in the bowl that was previously reserved. After pouring the dressing on top, give everything a good shake to incorporate.

Dinner Recipes

Cajun Air Fryer Salmon Two salmon fillets

Preparation time: 10 minutes **Cooking time: 15 minutes** **Serving: 2**

Nutrition:

- Calories: 400
- Carbs: 20g
- Protein: 19g
- Fats: 7g

Ingredients

- Cooking spray
- 1 tablespoon Cajun seasoning
- 1 milligram of dark brown sugar

Directions

1. Prepare the air fryer by heating it to 390 degrees Fahrenheit (200 degrees C).
2. The salmon fillets need to be washed and then dried with a paper towel. Cooking spray should be used to coat the fillets. In a low-volume dish, mix together the Cajun spice and the brown sugar. Spread evenly on a dish. Fillets should have the fleshy sides pressed into the seasoning mixture.
3. Cooking spray is sprayed into the basket of the air fryer, then salmon fillets with the skin side down are placed within. Spray the salmon one more with the cooking spray in a thin mist.
4. Wait 8 minutes before serving. Remove from the air fryer and allow rest for 2 minutes before serving.

Mexican-Style Stuffed Chicken Breasts Prepared in an Air Fryer

Preparation time: 15 minutes **Cooking time: 25 mint** **Serving: 2**

Nutrition:

- Calories: 180
- Carbs: 27g
- Protein: 19g
- Fats: 7g

Ingredients

- 4 exceptionally long toothpicks.
- a total of four tablespoons worth of chili powder, split
- Cumin ground to the equivalent of four teaspoons, divided
- 1 breast of chicken devoid of both skin and bones
- a couple of tablespoons' worth of chipotle flakes
- 2 tablespoons of oregano from Mexico
- To taste, salt, and freshly ground black pepper.
- 12 of red bell pepper, chopped lengthwise into very thin strips
- 1/2 of an onion, chopped lengthwise into very thin strips
- 1 fresh jalapeño, cut lengthwise into very thin strips
- 2 teaspoons of corn oil (corn oil)
- ½ lime, juiced

Directions

1. If you want to prevent toothpicks from catching fire while you're cooking, put them in a small basin, cover them with water, and let them soak.
2. On a plate of the same size, combine two teaspoons of chili powder and two teaspoons of cumin.
3. Prepare an air fryer by heating it to 400 degrees Fahrenheit (200 degrees C).
4. Place the chicken breasts on a completely flat work surface. Cut horizontally across the center of the item. Use a kitchen mallet or rolling pin to pound each half until it is about a quarter of an inch thick.
5. The remaining chili powder, cumin, chipotle flakes, oregano, salt, and pepper should be distributed evenly over both halves of each breast. Put one-half of each of the chopped bell pepper, onion, and jalapeño in the middle of one of the breast halves. After securing it with two toothpicks, roll the chicken starting from the pointy end and moving upward. Repeat the process with the remaining pieces of chicken breast, seasonings, and veggies, then fasten with the remaining toothpicks. While doing so, roll each roll-up in the chili-cumin mixture that is located in the shallow dish. Continue doing so until each roll-up is equally coated.
6. Position the roll-ups in the basket of the air fryer so that the side with the toothpicks is facing up. Set timer for 6 minutes.

7. To serve, flip the roll-ups over. Cooking should be continued for an additional 5 minutes in the air fryer until the juices flow clear and an instant-read thermometer put into the middle registers at least 165 degrees Fahrenheit (74 degrees Celsius).
8. Before serving, drizzle the roll-ups with lime juice in a uniform layer.

Turkey Breast Prepared in an Air Fryer

Preparation time: 15 minutes **Cooking time: 25 minutes** **Serving: 2**

Nutrition:

- Calories: 140
- Carbs: 25g
- Protein: 14g
- Fats: 6g

Ingredients

- 1 teaspoon of fresh rosemary that has been coarsely chopped
- 1 teaspoon of fresh chives that have been coarsely chopped
- 1 teaspoon of fresh garlic that has been freshly minced
- ½ teaspoon salt, or to taste
- 1/4 teaspoon of black pepper in ground form, or more to taste
- 2 tablespoons of butter, unsalted and cool.
- 2 pounds of bone-in, skin-on turkey breast

Directions

1. The air fryer should be preheated to 350 degrees F. (175 degrees C).
2. On a chopping board, arrange the rosemary, chives, garlic, and seasonings of your choice. On top of the herbs and spices, cut the butter into thin slices, and then mash everything together until it is well combined.
3. After patting the turkey breast dry, massage it all over with herb-infused butter, including beneath the skin.
4. Put the turkey into the basket of the air fryer with the skin-side facing down, and let it cook for twenty minutes.
5. After turning the turkey over so that the skin is facing up, continue to cook it for another 18 minutes, or until an instant-read thermometer placed near the bone registers 165 degrees Fahrenheit (74 degrees Celsius). Place the meat on a dish, cover it with aluminum foil, and let it sit for ten minutes before serving. Cut into pieces and serve hot.

Baby Back Ribs Cooked in an Air Fryer

Preparation time: 10 minutes **Cooking time: 15 minutes** **Serving: 1**

Nutrition:

- Calories: 100
- Carbs: 28g
- Protein: 28g
- Fats: 7 g

Ingredients

- 1 rack of baby back ribs in the bone
- 1 tablespoon olive oil
- 1 tablespoon liquid smoke flavoring
- 1 teaspoonful of dark brown sugar
- ½ teaspoon salt
- 1/2 teaspoon of black pepper in ground form
- 1/2 teaspoon of dried minced garlic
- 1/2 milligram of onion powder
- 1/2 teaspoon of ground chili peppers
- 1 cup BBQ sauce

Directions

1. The membrane should be removed from the rear of the ribs, and then the ribs should be dried with a paper towel. The rack should be cut into four equal halves. Rub the ribs on both sides with a mixture of olive oil and liquid smoke that has been combined in a small dish.
2. Brown sugar, salt, pepper, garlic powder, onion powder, and chili powder should all be mixed together in the same bowl. Apply a large amount of spice mix on both the meaty and the fattier side of the ribs. Resting the ribs for thirty minutes can help bring out their full taste.
3. Prepare an air fryer by heating it to 375 degrees Fahrenheit (190 degrees C).
4. When using an air fryer, place the ribs bone-side down in the basket and make sure they are not touching one another. If required, cook the ribs in batches.
5. Prepare food for fifteen minutes. Cook for a further ten minutes after turning the ribs over so that the meaty side is facing down. After removing the ribs from the air fryer, brush them on the bone side with a half cup of barbecue sauce. Return the basket to the air fryer and continue cooking for another 5 minutes. After turning the ribs over, spray the meat side with the remaining half cup of barbecue sauce and continue cooking for another 5 minutes or until the desired char is reached.

Meatloaf

Preparation time: 15 minutes **Cooking time: 20 minutes** **Serving: 2**

Nutrition:

- Calories: 140
- Carbs: 25g
- Protein: 14g
- Fats: 6g

Ingredients

- 1 pound of beef that has been leanly ground
- 1 very little onion, cut very finely
- 1 big egg, gently beaten
- 3 tablespoons of breadcrumbs in their dry form
- 1 teaspoon of fresh thyme that has been chopped
- 1 teaspoon salt
- freshly ground black pepper to your liking
- 2 mushrooms, cut into a thick layer
- 1 teaspoon of olive oil, more or less to taste

Directions

1. Prepare an air fryer by heating it to 392 degrees Fahrenheit (200 degrees C).
2. In a bowl, mix together the ground beef with the onion, breadcrumbs, thyme, egg, and some salt and pepper. Perform extensive kneading and mixing. Place the mixture inside a little loaf pan. After you have smoothed the top and pressed in the mushrooms, coat them with olive oil.
3. Cook the meatloaf in an air fryer that has been warmed until it is beautifully browned, which should take around 25 minutes. If you place an instant-read thermometer into the middle, it should register at least 165 degrees Fahrenheit (72 degrees C).
4. The meatloaf should be let to rest for at least ten minutes before being sliced into wedges and served.

Breaded Pork Chops Cooked in an Air Fryer

Preparation time: 15 minutes **Cooking time: 25 minutes** **Serving: 2**

Nutrition:

- Calories: 140
- Carbs: 25g
- Protein: 14g
- Fats: 6g

Ingredients

- 4 pork chops, boneless and center-cut, weighing 5 ounces each, with a thickness of 1 inch
- 1 teaspoon Cajun seasoning
- 1 and 12 cups of croutons topped with cheese and garlic.
- 2 big eggs
- Spray for cooking

Directions

1. Prepare an air fryer by heating it to 400 degrees Fahrenheit (200 degrees C).
2. Cajun spice should be applied on both sides of the pork chops that are placed on the platter.
3. Croutons should be ground up in a little food processor until they reach a fine consistency, then transferred to a shallow plate. In a separate, shallow dish, give the eggs a quick beat with a fork. When working one at a time, dip pork chops into beaten egg, allowing excess to drip off. Then, press pork chops into crouton breading to cover both sides, and lay breaded pork chops on a platter without stacking them. Continue in this manner with the remaining chops. Chops should be sprayed with cooking spray.
4. Spray the basket of the air fryer with cooking spray, then put the pork chops in the basket in a single layer. Cook the chops according to the manufacturer's instructions. Depending on the capacity of your air fryer, you may need to complete the process in two separate batches.
5. Once five minutes in the air fryer after it has been prepared, turn the chops over and spray them with cooking spray once more if there are any dry spots. Cook for 5 minutes more. The pork chops should reach an internal temperature of 145 degrees Fahrenheit when measured with an instant-read thermometer (63 degrees C).

AIR FRIED TERIYAKI PORK CHOPS

Preparation time: 15 minutes **Cooking time: 25 minutes** **Serving: 2**

Nutrition:

- Calories: 180
- Carbs: 27g
- Protein: 19g
- Fats: 7g

Ingredients

- 4 chops cut from the pork loin, 12 to 34 inches in thickness
- 2 tablespoons worth of horseradish sauce
- ⅓ cup Teriyaki marinade and sauce
- 1/4 milligram of cinnamon

Method

1. Mix together the horseradish sauce, the teriyaki sauce, and the cinnamon.
2. After pouring the sauce into a Ziploc bag, add the pork chops and shake well. After you have sealed the bag, shake it so that the pork chops are evenly coated with the sauce.
3. Put the bag in the fridge and let the pork chops marinate in the sauce for at least half an hour and up to a full hour.
4. After allowing them to marinate for the specified amount of time, remove them from the bag and place them in the air fryer. (Retain the sauce so that you can brush more of it onto the chops after you have flipped them. After that, throw away any leftover sauce.)
5. Cook in an air fryer at a temperature of 400 degrees Fahrenheit for 6–8 minutes per side. The internal temperature of pork chops should be brought up to 145 degrees.

Air-Fried Chicken Fajitas in the Air Fryer

Preparation time: 10 minutes **Cooking time: 20 minutes** **Serving: 2**

Nutrition:

- Calories: 100
- Carbs: 28g
- Protein: 28g
- Fats: 7 g

Ingredients

- Three boneless, skinless breasts of chicken
- 1 red bell pepper
- 1 orange bell pepper
- 1 yellow bell pepper in total
- 1 onion
- Seasoning for tacos, four tablespoons

Method

1. Bring the temperature of the Air Fryer up to 380 degrees Fahrenheit. After the preheat cycle of the Air Fryer is finished, you should spray the basket with nonstick spray and get it ready.
2. Cut the chicken and each of the vegetables into thin slices. Put the slices in a bowl of a suitable size, and then sprinkle the taco seasoning over them.
3. Cook the chicken and vegetables for 18 minutes at a temperature of 380 degrees Fahrenheit, after adding the seasoning to the basket of the prepared air fryer. To ensure that everything cooks at the same rate, you should stir the chicken and the vegetables every few minutes.
4. After removing the chicken and vegetables from the Air Fryer, serve them with flour tortillas, cheese, and any other fajita toppings that you enjoy.

Air Fryer Honey Garlic Chicken Wings

Preparation time: 10 minutes **Cooking time: 30 minutes** **Serving: 2**

Nutrition:

- Calories:140
- Carbs: 25g
- Protein: 14g
- Fats: 6g

Ingredients

- 1/5 chicken wings, separated into the wings and drumsticks.
- ½ cup olive oil
- 4 milliliters of minced garlic
- 1 level tablespoon of granulated sugar
- 1 tbsp sriracha sauce
- 1 tbsp margarine
- 4 tablespoons of low-sodium soy sauce
- 1 half cup of honey
- 1 half cup of water
- 1 teaspoon of cornstarch
- 1 tablespoon of toasted sesame seeds

Method

1. Bring the temperature of the Air Fryer up to 360 degrees Fahrenheit.
2. Prepare the chicken wings by cutting them into dummies and small wings, then placing them in a plastic storage bag. After adding the olive oil and sealing the bag, toss the wings around until they are completely coated in the seasoning.
3. Cook the wings in the air fryer for 18 minutes, making sure to place them in a single layer in the prepared basket. Turn the wings over once every six minutes. After 18 minutes, set the temperature of the air fryer to 390 degrees Fahrenheit for an additional two minutes of cooking time, bringing the total amount of time spent cooking to a total of 20 minutes.
4. During the time that the wings are in the oven, place the remaining ingredients in a small saucepan and bring them to a boil. Reduce the heat to low and allow the sauce to gently simmer for ten minutes while stirring it frequently. Take the sauce off the heat and cover it to keep it warm.
5. After the wings have been cooked, place them in a bowl with a medium-sized mixing spoon, pour the wing sauce over them, and use the spoon to toss them until they are completely covered.
6. Just before serving, transfer the wings to a serving platter and sprinkle them with the toasted sesame seeds.
7. Before cooking, add a pinch of baking powder to each wing, and then cook the wings. This will make the wings extra crispy.

8. Before serving, check that the wings have reached an internal temperature of at least 165 degrees Fahrenheit on a food thermometer. If necessary, add one-to-two-minute increments of additional cooking time.
9. Keep any leftover wings in a container that seals tightly and places them in the refrigerator for up to three days. To reheat the chicken, turn on the air fryer and set the temperature to 390 degrees Fahrenheit. Cook the chicken for three to five minutes, or until it is hot all the way through.

Air Fryer Swai Fish

Preparation time: 15 minutes **Cooking time: 25 minutes** **Serving: 2**

Nutrition:

- Calories: 100
- Carbs: 28g
- Protein: 28g
- Fats: 7 g

Ingredients

- 2/4 ounce Swai fillets
- 1 milliliter of olive oil with a dash of blackened seasoning to taste

Method

1. Bring the temperature of the Air Fryer up to 390 degrees Fahrenheit. Prepare the basket of the air fryer by spraying it with olive oil, a non-stick cooking spray, or parchment paper.
2. The fish fillets should be coated with olive oil on both sides before cooking. A coating of blackened seasoning should be applied to both sides of the fish.
3. Once the fish fillets have been coated, place them in the basket of the air fryer and set the timer for five minutes. After that, flip the fillets and set the timer for three more minutes.
4. Include your go-to side dish in the serving. Maintain a healthy diet by selecting options such as salad, sweet potatoes, or fresh vegetables.

Ribeye Steak

Preparation time: 15 miniutes **Cooking time: 25 minutes** **Serving: 2**

Nutrition:

- Calories:140
- Carbs: 25g
- Protein: 14g
- Fats: 6g

Ingredients

- 2 rib-eye steaks that are each 16 ounces in weight
- 1 tablespoon olive oil
- ½ teaspoon pepper
- ½ teaspoon salt
- Blue Cheese Butter
- 2 tbsp unsalted butter melted
- 1 level tablespoon of crumbled blue cheese

Method

1. Served with a topping of butter and blue cheese
2. In the microwave, for approximately 30 seconds, melt the butter and blue cheese together to make the butter topping. Mix everything thoroughly, then put it back in the refrigerator while the steak is cooking.
3. After giving the steak a thin coating of olive oil on both sides, season it with salt and pepper, or any other seasonings you like.
4. Set the temperature on the air fryer to 400 degrees Fahrenheit.
5. Cook at 400 degrees Fahrenheit for six to eight minutes on each side, depending on the degree of doneness that you prefer.
6. Allow the steak to rest for 5–10 minutes before serving, then dollop a spoonful of the prepared butter on top.
7. Before serving, allow the steak to rest in the juices for five to ten minutes.
8. Weight Watchers: Approximately seven points are assigned to four ounces of ribeye steak; if you serve it with steak sauce, you can add the point.

Lobster Tails for the Air Fryer

Preparation time: 10 minutes **Cooking time: 15 minutes** **Serving: 1**

Nutrition:

- Calories: 180
- Carbs: 27g
- Protein: 19g
- Fats: 7g

Ingredients

- 2 tails of lobster weighing between 6 and 8 ounces each
- 2 tablespoons unsalted butter melted
- 2 cloves of garlic, chopped or pressed, minced
- 1 teaspoon lemon juice
- ½ teaspoon salt and pepper
- 1 quarter of a teaspoon of old bay seasoning

Method

1. Cut in the very top of the shell of each lobster until you can gently pull the meat up so that it rests on the shell.
2. Make cuts in the meat with a knife but be careful not to go all the way through.
3. Position the lobster tails in the basket of the air fryer. (Parchment paper lining is an optional step.)
4. Mix together the garlic, lemon juice, and seasonings with the melted butter. Mix everything together. Use a brush to apply the mixture on top of each lobster, covering the meat.
5. Cook at 380 degrees Fahrenheit for six to eight minutes.
6. At the halfway point, brush the meat with some additional butter.
7. This meal can be made to count as zero points by exchanging the salted butter for Countryside Creamery's Tastes like Butter Spray.

Air Fryer BBQ Chicken Wings

Preparation time: 15 minutes **Cooking time: 25 minutes** **Serving: 2**

Nutrition:

- Calories:140
- Carbs: 25g
- Protein: 14g
- Fats: 6g

Ingredients

- 2/4 chicken wings
- 1 Tbsp. garlic powder
- 2 tablespoons of dark sugar
- ⅔ Cup BBQ sauce

Method

1. Bring the temperature of the Air Fryer up to 380 degrees Fahrenheit. AFTER you have preheated the Air Fryer, you should prepare the basket by spraying it with olive oil spray, a nonstick cooking spray, or lining it with parchment paper.
2. After being washed and patted dry, the chicken wings are ready to be used.
3. Create a dry rub by combining the garlic powder and brown sugar in equal parts, then apply it to the wings. Before coating the wings in the seasoning, add a dash of baking powder to achieve wings that are even crispier than usual.
4. In the basket of the air fryer, arrange the chicken wings in a single layer.
5. Cook the wings in an oven preheated to 380 degrees Fahrenheit for 16 minutes, turning them over once every four minutes. Cook for an additional four minutes after the temperature was raised to 400 degrees Fahrenheit. Employing a meat thermometer, check that the wings have reached an internal temperature of 165 degrees Fahrenheit. If there is a need, add one to two minutes to the time.
6. Take the chicken wings out of the air fryer and place them in a mixing bowl that's about the size of a medium-sized bowl. Apply some barbecue sauce to the chicken wings, and then toss them so that the sauce covers all of the wings completely.
7. Serve with the sides and dipping sauces that you enjoy the most.
8. You can serve the wings with additional barbecue sauce or any of your preferred dipping sauces, such as honey mustard or creamy Ranch dressing.
9. If you want the wings to have an even crispier exterior, add a pinch of baking powder to the seasoning.

Chicken Parmesan

Preparation time: 15 minutes **Cooking time: 25 minutes** **Serving: 2**

Nutrition:

- Calories: 180
- Carbs: 27g
- Protein: 19g
- Fats: 7g

Ingredients

- 2 chicken breasts that have been cut in half
- ½ cup breadcrumbs
- ½ cup panko
- 1 half cup of grated parmesan cheese
- 2 tablespoons of dried Italian seasoning
- 2 eggs
- 4 Tbsp. marinara sauce
- 4 Tbsp. mozzarella cheese

Method

1. Bring the temperature of the Air Fryer up to 350 degrees Fahrenheit.
2. Take the two chicken breasts and cut them in half horizontally. Make the chicken breasts approximately half an inch to an inch in thickness by pounding them with a meat masher.
3. Panko, breadcrumbs, and Italian spice should all be combined in a separate bowl. In a separate dish, combine the eggs by whisking them.
4. After dredging the chicken in the breadcrumb mixture, each piece of chicken should be dipped in the egg mixture. Arrange them in a single row on the basket of the air fryer that has been previously prepared.
5. Combine the mozzarella and parmesan in a low-volume bowl for easy mixing.
6. Prepare the chicken by cooking it for seven minutes at 350 degrees Fahrenheit. Place one tablespoon of marinara sauce and one tablespoon of the combination of mozzarella and parmesan cheese on top of each piece of chicken. Put the basket back into the air fryer and continue the cooking process for another 5 minutes.
7. Prepare with the sides that you choose.
8. This dish was prepared with the help of a Cosori air fryer. Every Air Fryer has a unique cooking method. The wattage of your Air Fryer may be different from mine, which will cause the cooking time for this dish to be either longer or shorter. If the power wattage of your air fryer is lower than what the recipe calls for, you may need to increase the total cooking time.

9. Keep any leftover chicken parmesan in a jar that seals tightly and puts it in the refrigerator for up to three days. Reheat the chicken in an air fryer set to 350 degrees for two minutes, or until it reaches an internal temperature of 165 degrees.
10. When you're ready to eat, accompany the chicken parmesan with a serving of spaghetti noodles, Alfredo noodles, zucchini noodles, or roasted veggies.
11. You may serve the leftovers with the sides you like most, or you can make a chicken parmesan sandwich with the leftovers by placing them on a bun.

Buffalo Chicken Wings Baked In the Air Fryer

Preparation time: 15 minutes **Cooking time: 25 minutes** **Serving: 2**

Nutrition:

- Calories: 100
- Carbs: 28g
- Protein: 28g
- Fats: 7 g

Ingredient

- 24 wings
- 1 cup olive oil
- a tablespoon's worth of ground black pepper
- 2 milligrams of onion powder
- 2 milligrams of garlic powder
- Buffalo Wing Sauce
- 1 mug of Hot Sauce from Louisiana
- ½ cup margarine
- 4 tbsp. water
- 2 tsp. paprika
- a quarter teaspoon of granulated sugar
- 1/4 of a teaspoon of garlic powder
- 1/4 milligram of onion powder

Method

1. Put the Air Fryer into the oven and preheat it to 360 degrees Fahrenheit. Get ready to assemble the basket.
2. Place the chicken wings, olive oil, and spices inside a big plastic bag that can be sealed. After you have sealed the bag, open it up and toss the wings to equally distribute the oil and spices.
3. After the air fryer basket has been prepared, arrange the wings in a single layer inside of it. Cook the wings at a temperature of 360 degrees for 18 minutes, turning them over every 5–6 minutes. Raise the temperature to 390 degrees Fahrenheit and continue to cook for another two minutes. Before removing the wings from the oven, use the meat thermometer to check that they have reached 165 degrees Fahrenheit.

Wing sauce

1. Put all of the ingredients for the sauce into a saucepan and start heating them over a medium flame. After bringing the contents of the wing sauce to a boil, remove it as fast as possible from the heat, and then cover it with a lid to let it sit for 5 minutes.
2. After the wings have finished cooking, place them in a dish of suitable size and top them with the sauce. To ensure that the wings are fully coated, give them a quick toss before removing them and placing them on a platter.
3. Prepare with the dipping sauce of your choice and serve.
4. Before beginning the frying process, add a little bit of baking powder to the chicken wings so that they become extremely crispy.

5. Think about adding variety to the tastes by using a variety of dipping sauces. The Marie's Creamy Ranch dressing is the one that I like eating most with these chicken wings.
6. The leftover chicken wings may be kept in the refrigerator for up to three days if they are sealed in an airtight container. Reheat the wings in the Air Fryer set to 390 degrees for two to three minutes, or until they have reached the desired level of rewarming.

Chicken Street Tacos Made In the Air Fryer

Preparation time: 10 minutes **Cooking time: 15 minutes** **Serving: 1**

Nutrition:

- Calories: 140
- Carbs: 25g
- Protein: 14g
- Fats: 6g

Ingredients

- 1 tablespoon of olive oil.
- 1 pound of chicken breasts that have been sliced into strips.
- 2 milligrams of chili powder
- 1 tsp salt
- ½ tsp black pepper
- 1/2 flour tortillas (four inches in size)
- **Toppings**
- Onion
- Lettuce
- Tomatoes
- Cheese
- Cream Fraiche

Method

1. Olive oil should be used to lightly brush the air fryer basket.
2. Place the pieces of raw chicken in a medium bowl and season them with the chili powder, salt, and pepper using a tossing motion until all of the chicken pieces are evenly covered with the ingredients.
3. Put the chicken into the basket that has been made, and air-fried it at 380 degrees Fahrenheit for 5 minutes. After that, flip the chicken over, and continue air frying at 380 degrees for another 5 minutes.
4. Place on top of street taco tortillas and garnish with any other toppings you want.

Parmesan-Crusted Chicken Done In the Air Fryer

Preparation time: 10 minutes **Cooking time: 15 minutes** **Serving: 1**

Nutrition:

- Calories: 180
- Carbs: 27g
- Protein: 19g
- Fats: 7g

Ingredients

- 2/8 oz breast meat from boneless, skinless chicken
- 2 tbsp sour cream
- 1/4 cup Panko Breadcrumbs in an Italian Style
- 1/4 cup of parmesan cheese that has been grated
- ½ teaspoon paprika
- ¼ teaspoon salt
- ¼ teaspoon pepper
- 1 tablespoon olive oil

Method

1. Bring the internal temperature of the air fryer up to 380 degrees Fahrenheit.
2. After rinsing the chicken, blot it dry using paper towels.
3. Spread one spoonful of sour cream or Greek yogurt on top of each piece of chicken, making sure that you just cover the tops of the chicken.
4. Mix the panko, grated Parmesan cheese, and spices together in a basin of medium size.
5. Spread the cheese mixture over the sour cream using a patting motion.
6. Apply a thin layer of olive oil to the basket by spraying it or brushing it on.
7. Cook the chicken for 12 minutes at 380 degrees Fahrenheit, having first placed it in the basket.
8. Flip the chicken over and return it to the fryer for a further 4-6 minutes of cooking time. The amount of time needed may vary based on the thickness of the chicken.

Pistachio-Crusted Chicken Prepared In an Air Fryer

Preparation time: 15 minutes **Cooking time: 25 minutes** **Serving: 2**

Nutrition:

- Calories: 100
- Carbs: 28g
- Protein: 28g
- Fats: 7 g

Ingredients

- 2 chicken breasts, boneless and skinless, weighing a total of 2.6 ounces
- ½ teaspoon salt
- ¼ teaspoon pepper
- 2 tbsp. mayonnaise
- 12 cups of pistachios that have been roasted and salted
- 1 tablespoon olive oil

Method

1. Sprinkle desired amounts of salt and pepper all over each chicken breast.
2. Spread one tablespoon of mayonnaise on top of each piece, covering the tops as well as the edges of each piece. There is no need to be concerned about the underside of the bird.
3. Each piece should be topped with one-fourth of a cup of chopped pistachios, and the mayonnaise should be softly pressed into the pistachios until the whole piece is covered.
4. Prepare at a temperature of 370 degrees Fahrenheit for fifteen to eighteen minutes, depending on the thickness.
5. If you are cooking more than two chicken breasts at once, divide the mayonnaise and pistachios evenly among the pieces, using one tablespoon of mayonnaise and a quarter cup of chopped nuts for each chicken breast. Adjust seasonings according to taste.
6. The thickness of the chicken will determine whether or not the cooking times need to be modified.
7. A temperature of 165 degrees Fahrenheit should be maintained within the chicken.
8. If you follow the Weight Watchers program, you may reduce the number of points you need to worry about by using low-fat mayonnaise or sour cream.

Chicken Prepared In an Air Fryer

Preparation time: 10 minutes **Cooking time: 15 minutes** **Serving: 1**

Nutrition:

- Calories:140
- Carbs: 25g
- Protein: 14g
- Fats: 6g

Ingredients

- 1 Chicken (Whole) about 4-5 Pounds
- 1 tablespoon of the Italian spice blend
- ½ tsp. Paprika
- 1/2 milligrams of ground black pepper

Method

1. Put the Air Fryer into the oven and preheat it to 360 degrees Fahrenheit. After the basket has been heated, prepare the liner by spraying it with a cooking spray that prevents sticking.
2. It is important to clean the chicken and remove any innards that may be found within the bird's cavity. The chicken should be well coated in the spices before cooking.
3. Cook the chicken for 25 minutes after placing it with the breast side down in the prepared basket for the Air Fryer and seasoning it. After that, turn the chicken over so that the breast side is facing up and continue to cook it for another 40 minutes.
4. Check the temperature by placing a thermometer into the section of the chicken breast that is the thickest before taking the chicken out of the oven. You are allowed to remove the food from the Air Fryer after the temperature reaches at least 165 degrees Fahrenheit. If this is not the case, continue cooking for an additional two minutes, or until the temperature reaches 165 degrees.
5. The leftover chicken may be kept in the refrigerator for up to three days if it is stored in an airtight container.
6. Reheat any chicken that has been left over in the Air Fryer at a temperature of 280 degrees Fahrenheit for eight to ten minutes, or until the chicken is completely reheated.
7. Make use of any leftover chicken by cooking up some additional recipes and prepping some meals.

Air Fryer Honey Mustard Salmon

Preparation time: 15 minutes **Cooking time: 20 minutes** **Serving: 2**

Nutrition:

- Calories: 180
- Carbs: 27g
- Protein: 19g
- Fats: 7g

Ingredients

- 2-4 servings of Salmon 4-6 ounces each
- 1 tablespoon olive oil ½ teaspoon salt ½ teaspoon pepper
- 2 tbsp. Dijon Mustard
- 1 1/2 teaspoons of honey

Method

1. Olive oil should be applied to the bottom of the basket using either a brush or a spray bottle
2. Place the salmon chunks in the basket, and then season them with salt & pepper to taste.
3. Combine the honey and Dijon mustard in a low-volume bowl and swirl to combine.
4. Apply the honey mustard mixture to the tops of each chunk of salmon using a pastry brush or a spoon. Ensure that the coating is uniform.
5. Cook for 10 to 12 minutes at a temperature of 380 degrees Fahrenheit with the basket covered.
6. Use a fork to determine if the food is done. Immediately serve after cooking.

Taco Casserole Made In the Air Fryer

Preparation time: 15 minutes **Cooking time: 25 minutes** **Serving: 2**

Nutrition:

- Calories:140
- Carbs: 25g
- Protein: 14g
- Fats: 6g

Ingredients

- 1 pound of lean ground beef, of which 95% is lean
- 3 tablespoons worth of taco seasoning
- 1/4 mug of water
- 12 cups of chopped red bell pepper
- 10 ounces of chopped tomatoes and green chilies, none of which have been drained
- 4 big eggs
- ¼ cup sour cream
- 13 cups of full-fat heavy cream
- ½ cup cheddar cheese shredded
- Optional: 1 tablespoon of chopped green onions

Method

1. In a pan set over medium heat, brown the lean ground beef for about five minutes, or until it is no longer pink.
2. The water, taco seasoning, chopped bell pepper, and canned tomatoes with green chilies should all be added now. While stirring, simmer for the next three minutes.
3. Put the Air Fryer into the oven and preheat it to 300 degrees Fahrenheit. Get the casserole or cake dish ready for the air fryer.
4. Eggs, sour cream, and heavy cream should be combined and whisked together in a medium-sized mixing basin. Set aside.
5. Place an even layer of the taco meat mixture in the bottom of the casserole dish that has been prepped. The egg mixture should be added on top of the meat mixture.
6. Cook the casserole in the air fryer for 18 minutes once it has been placed in the basket. Add the cheese on top, then continue cooking for another two minutes, or until the cheese has completely melted.
7. Add some green onions on top, then serve.
8. To keep for up to three days, place it in a refrigerator-safe container that seals tightly and store it.
9. Consider using other seasonings, such as sliced jalapenos for an added kick of heat.
10. To give the meal a more interesting taste profile, add a little mozzarella and cream cheese to the mixture.

Catfish cooked in an air fryer

Preparation time: 15 minutes **Cooking time: 25 minutes** **Serving: 2**

Nutrition:

- Calories: 178
- Carbs: 45g
- Protein: 1g
- Fats: 1g

Ingredients

- 1 pound of fillets of catfish
- 1 cup of breading for fish fry
- 1 lemon, sliced into wedges, and 1 tablespoon of olive oil.

Method

1. 5 minutes should be spent getting the Air Fryer up to a temperature of 400 degrees Fahrenheit.
2. Before coating, make sure the catfish has been well-washed and dried with paper towels. Put the seasoned breadcrumbs in a basin that's not too deep, and then dip each piece of fish in the bowl until it's fully covered. A little coating of olive oil cooking spray should be applied to each fillet.
3. Place fillets in the Air Fryer basket in a single layer once it has been prepared. After ten minutes of cooking at 400 degrees, gently turn the catfish fillets over and continue to cook them for another ten minutes. To make them super crispy, you will need to flip them one more time and cook them for an additional one to two minutes.
4. Coleslaw, air-fried French fries, air-fried hush puppies, and tartar sauce should be served with the fish. Just before serving, drizzle the fillets with fresh lemon juice that has been squeezed from a lemon.
5. Notes If you are searching for more air fryer fish recipes that have a mild taste and can be prepared in a short amount of time, you can think about using other varieties of white fish such as tilapia, bass, haddock, grouper, and snapper fish.
6. The Louisiana brand fish fry is my favorite, but if you want to create your handmade version, that's always an option. They should be seasoned with cornmeal, flour, Cajun spice, salt, pepper, and a seafood seasoning like Old Bay. Before frying, dredge the fish in the cornmeal mixture that has been prepared. The Louisiana Cajun catfish fry is one of my favorites but is warned: it's spicy! Try that one as well if you don't mind things being on the hot side.
7. When I prepare catfish fillets, I rarely cut them into strips because I like to leave them whole. The total cooking time for my catfish fillets is going to be twenty-two minutes. The catfish will get an additional two minutes of cooking time for an exceptionally crispy crust.

Nachos Prepared in an Air Fryer

Preparation time: 15 minutes **Cooking time: 25 minutes** **Serving: 2**

Nutrition:

- Calories: 500
- Carbs: 23g
- Protein: 8g
- Fats: 0g

Ingredients

- 2 measuring cups of nacho chips
- 1 half a cup of chicken fajita meat a half a cup of sliced cherry tomatoes
- 1 measure and a half of shredded cheese
- 1 quarter of a cup of black olives
- 1/4 cup sliced jalapeno

Methods

1. Prepare the tray of the air fryer by spraying it with a nonstick spray, such as olive oil. Arrange the nacho chips in a layer at the bottom of the basket of the air fryer.
2. The chips should be topped with fajita meat, cheese, tomatoes, and jalapenos that have been sliced.
3. After three to five minutes of cooking at a temperature of 320 degrees Fahrenheit, check on the nachos every two minutes to verify that the cheese has melted and that the tops of the chips have become a light golden-brown color.
4. Take the nachos out of the Air Fryer and place them on a serving dish. Top the nachos with the toppings of your choice, such as a dab of sour cream, sliced avocado, sliced black olives, and salsa.
5. Before beginning this dish, I did not preheat the Air Fryer.
6. You may replace fajita chicken meat with ground beef, fajita steak strips, ground turkey, or ground beef that has been seasoned with taco seasoning. Rotisserie chicken is another option.
7. Use toppings for nachos in addition to those listed above, such as black beans, bell pepper, corn, refried beans, green onions, fresh cilantro, and diced tomatoes with green chilies.
8. The nachos may be kept in the refrigerator for up to three days if they are sealed in an airtight container. Sprinkle more cheese on top of the nachos, then microwave the mixture for two to three minutes.
9. I like to have my basket ready before preparing the nachos so that the clean-up is less of a hassle. At the bottom of the basket, you might use olive oil spray, parchment paper, or even aluminum foil.

Air Fryer Steak Kabobs

Preparation time: 10 minutes **Cooking time:** 15 minutes **Serving:** 1

Nutrition:

- Calories: 180
- Carbs: 27g
- Protein: 19g
- Fats: 7g

Ingredients

- 1/5 oz steak
- 1 red bell pepper
- 1 green bell pepper
- 1 red onion 1 tablespoon of olive oil
- 2 tablespoons of soy sauce

Methods

1. Prepare the Air Fryer by setting the temperature to 400 degrees Fahrenheit. Prepare the basket of the Air Fryer by spraying it with a spray that prevents food from sticking, such as olive oil or avocado oil.
2. While you are chopping the veggies, cut the steak into bite-sized pieces, and then soak those pieces in the soy sauce.
3. To make the bell peppers and onions easier to eat, cut them into smaller pieces.
4. Take a skewer and add the steak, onion, and peppers in a rotating fashion, doing so until you have reached the end of the skewer, and then repeat the process.
5. In the prepared basket for the Air Fryer, arrange the steak skewers so that they form a single layer. Cook for ten minutes at 400 degrees Fahrenheit, turning the skewers over halfway through the cooking time.
6. You may serve it on its own, with a dipping sauce, or with the sides you want.
7. You may keep any leftovers in the refrigerator for up to three days if you place them in an airtight container. To reheat them, throw them in an air fryer that has been prepared to 400 degrees Fahrenheit and leave them there for three to four minutes, or until they are cooked completely through.
8. Your favorite cuts of steak are the greatest selection when it comes to red meat. When it comes to making the tastiest beef kebabs, top sirloin, ribeye, and New York strip steaks are my personal favorites. You may also use a cheaper piece of beef like stew meat in its place.
9. Make sure to use simple flavors like teriyaki sauce, soy sauce, and Worcestershire sauce. You also have the option of using garlic powder, steak spice, or onion powder.
10. Do you prefer chicken? You may substitute chicken for steak if

11. you want. Alternately, or in addition to the steak, you might replace it on the skewer with chicken breasts that have been cut up into bite-sized pieces using a cube cutter.

Chicken Breasts Prepared in an Air Fryer

Preparation time: 10 minutes   **Cooking time: 20 minutes**   **Serving: 2**

Nutrition:

- Calories: 100
- Carbs: 28g
- Protein: 28g
- Fats: 7 g

Ingredients

- 3 pieces of chicken breast (boneless skinless)
- 4 tablespoons of olive oil
- 3/4 cup breadcrumbs
- 1 milligram of white pepper
- 1 level tablespoon of garlic powder
- 1 level tablespoon of onion powder
- 1 tsp. black pepper

Method

1. Bring the temperature inside the air fryer up to 380 degrees.
2. Mix the breadcrumbs and the other spices together.
3. Olive oil should be used to coat the chicken breasts. Coat the chicken breasts in the combination of breadcrumbs and seasonings well before adding them to the mixture.
4. Spray the basket with cooking spray that prevents food from sticking, or insert a tiny layer of parchment paper. Cook the chicken for ten minutes after placing it in the basket, then spray it with olive oil spray and give it a light coating. After turning the chicken over, sprinkle it with a second layer of olive oil spray and continue to cook for another 10–12 minutes.
5. Verify that the chicken reaches an internal temperature of 165 degrees Fahrenheit throughout its thickest region by taking its temperature. If not, continue cooking for an additional two to four minutes, checking the temperature to make sure it reaches 165 degrees Fahrenheit and then removing the dish from the oven.
6. Take the chicken out of the air fryer and cover it with aluminum foil for the remaining five minutes before serving.
7. To enhance the taste of the chicken breasts before cooking them, marinate them.
8. Cooking times for chicken breasts may vary greatly depending on the size and weight of the bird. When I cook, I normally use chicken breasts of medium size, and I find that twenty minutes is the ideal amount of time to cook them. The cooking time required for a chicken breast of a smaller size will be less than that required for a breast of a bigger size. Depending on how much larger or smaller the item is, I will add or subtract one minute from the total cooking time.
9. Take, for example A small chicken breast weighing 8 ounces after cooking for twenty minutes, I will check the internal temperature before bringing out the food. Before taking the temperature, I will

cook a chicken breast that is either medium or nine ounces for twenty-two minutes. If it's a bigger chicken breast weighing 10 to 12 ounces, I'll cook it for 22 to 24 minutes, and I'll start monitoring the temperature on the inside of the breast at 20 minutes.

Pork Chops Cooked In an Air Fryer

Preparation time: 10 minutes **Cooking time: 15 minutes** **Serving: 1**

Nutrition:

- Calories: 140
- Carbs: 25g
- Protein: 14g
- Fats: 6g

Ingredients

- 3 pork chops of the thick-cut kind
- ½ tsp black pepper
- ¼ tsp paprika
- ¼ tsp garlic powder
- 1/4 milligram of onion powder

Method

1. Prepare the Air Fryer by setting the temperature to 400 degrees Fahrenheit.
2. Mix the ingredients together in a small bowl, and then use your hands to spread the seasoning all over the pork chops, being sure to coat all of the surfaces of each chop, including the front, back, and sides.
3. After spraying the inside of the Air Fryer basket with nonstick cooking spray or lining it with parchment paper, arrange the pork chops in a single layer across the base of the Air Fryer basket. Make sure there is enough space between each pork chop for air to circulate.
4. Cook for six minutes at 400 degrees Fahrenheit. After turning the pork chops over, continue cooking them for a further 8 to 10 minutes. Before taking the meat out of the oven, check with a meat thermometer to see whether the internal temperature has reached 145 degrees Fahrenheit. If more time is required, increase it in increments of two minutes.
5. As soon as possible, serve the sides that you choose.

Appetizers

Pickles Prepared in an Air Fryer

Preparation time: 15 minutes **Cooking time: 25 minutes** **Serving: 2**

Nutrition:

- Calories: 180
- Carbs: 27g
- Protein: 19g
- Fats: 7g

Ingredients

- 32 dill pickle slices
- 1/2 cup all-purpose flour
- 1/2 teaspoon salt
- 3 big eggs, whisked briefly to combine.
- 2 tablespoons dill pickle juice
- 1/2 milligrams of red pepper flakes
- 1/2 milligram of the garlic powder
- Panko bread crumbs equivalent to 2 cups
- 2 tablespoons of fresh dill, chopped into small pieces
- Cooking spray
- Dressing ranch salad with it if you so want.

Method

1. Bring the temperature of the air fryer to 400 degrees. Allow the pickles to sit on paper towels for about 15 minutes, or until virtually all of the liquid has been absorbed.
2. In the meanwhile, whisk together the flour and salt in a wide-mouthed basin. Eggs, pickle juice, cayenne pepper, and garlic powder should be whisked together in a separate shallow basin. In a third, shallower dish, mix together the panko and dill.
3. Coat the pickles on both sides with the flour mixture and then brush off any excess. After dipping in the egg mixture, transfer it to the crumb mixture and massage down to help the coating stick. Pickles should be spread out in a single layer on a greased pan and placed in the air fryer basket in batches. Cook for 7–10 minutes, or until the topping is golden brown and crispy. Pickles should be turned over and sprayed with frying spray. Continue cooking for a further 7-10 minutes, until the bacon is golden brown and crispy. Serve immediately, and if wanted, accompany with ranch dressing.

Air-Fryer Chicken Wings

Preparation time: 10 minutes **Cooking time: 15 minutes** **Serving: 1**

Nutrition:

- Calories:140
- Carbs: 25g
- Protein: 14g
- Fats: 6g

Ingredients

- 2 teaspoons of dried minced garlic
- 1 level teaspoon of salted garlic
- 1 teaspoon of powdered mustard, 1 teaspoon of ginger, and 1 teaspoon of nutmeg
- 1/2 teaspoon pepper
- Allspice, ground, one-half of a teaspoon
- 1/2 teaspoon baking soda
- 1/2 milligrams of red pepper flakes
- 12 complete chicken wings (and a half-pound and a half)

Optional:

- Buffalo sauce, Ranch salad dressing, or barbecue sauce are other examples.

Directions

1. Bring the temperature of the air fryer to 300 degrees. Garlic powder, garlic salt, mustard, ginger, nutmeg, pepper, allspice, baking soda, and cayenne pepper should be mixed together in a big basin.
2. Chicken wings should be cut into three parts, with the tip portions being discarded. Mix well after adding to the basin containing the seasonings. Prepare the wings by placing them in a single layer on a greased tray that has been placed inside the air fryer basket. Cook for 15 minutes. Raise the temperature to 400 degrees and continue cooking for 20 to 25 minutes, or until the chicken juices run clear and the wings are golden brown. Continue in the same manner with the remaining wings. Serve hot, and accompany with your preferred dressing or sauce.

Garlic Bread Prepared in an Air Fryer

Preparation time: 15 minutes **Cooking time: 25 minutes** **Serving: 2**

Nutrition:

- Calories: 178
- Carbs: 45g
- Protein: 1g
- Fats: 1g

Ingredients

- 1 quarter of a cup of butter, softened
- 3 tablespoons of parmesan cheese that has been grated
- 2 cloves of garlic, finely chopped
- 2 tablespoons of finely chopped fresh parsley or 1/2 teaspoon of parsley flakes that have been dried
- 8 slices of your choice:
- Ciabatta, French bread, or both

Directions

1. Bring the temperature of the air fryer to 350 degrees. Mix the first four ingredients together in a small dish, then distribute them on the bread.
2. Bread should be arranged in a single layer on the tray that is placed inside the air fryer basket. After two to three minutes, the food should be golden brown. To be served hot.

Air-Fryer Shrimp in a Sauce Made of Coconut and Apricots

Preparation time: 10 minutes **Cooking time: 15 minutes** **Serving: 2**

Nutrition:

- Calories: 140
- Carbs: 25g
- Protein: 14g
- Fats: 6g

Ingredients

- 1-and-one-half pounds of raw shrimp (26-30 per pound)
- 1-and-a-half cups of shredded sweetened coconut
- 1/2 cup panko breadcrumbs
- 4 egg whites from huge eggs
- 3 dashes of Louisiana-style spicy sauce
- 1/4 teaspoon salt
- 1/4 teaspoon pepper
- 1/2 cup all-purpose flour sauce:
- 1 cup apricot preserves
- 1 teaspoon cider vinegar
- 1 quarter of a teaspoon of red pepper flakes crushed

Directions

1. Heat the air fryer to 375 degrees. Shrimp should be peeled and deveined, but the tails should be left on.
2. Combine the shredded coconut and breadcrumbs in a small basin. Egg whites, spicy sauce, salt, and pepper should be whisked together in a separate shallow basin. Put the flour in the third basin, which is the shallowest one.
3. Shrimp should be gently coated with flour and then any excess flour should be shaken off. First, coat in the egg white mixture then rolls in the coconut mixture and pat to help the coating stick.
4. Place shrimp in a single layer on a greased tray and transfer the tray to the air fryer basket in batches. Cook for 4 minutes. After turning the shrimp over, continue to cook for approximately four more minutes, or until the coconut is gently browned and the shrimp become pink.
5. In the meanwhile, combine all of the ingredients for the sauce in a small saucepan. Cook the mixture while stirring it over medium-low heat until the preserves are completely melted. As soon as possible, serve the shrimp with the sauce.

Air-Fried Spinach and Feta

Preparation time: 15 minutes **Cooking time: 20 minutes** **Serving: 2**

Nutrition:

- Calories: 180
- Carbs: 27g
- Protein: 19g
- Fats: 7g

Ingredients

- 2 big eggs
- 1 thawed bag of frozen spinach, 10 ounces in total, cut after being wrung dry.
- 3/4 cup of feta cheese in crumbled form
- 2 cloves of garlic, finely chopped
- 1/4 teaspoon pepper
- 1 tube (13.8 ounces) (13.8 ounces) refrigerated pizza crust
- Refrigerated tzatziki sauce, optional

Directions

1. Bring the temperature of the air fryer to 425 degrees. Whisk the eggs in a dish; remove one tablespoon of the eggs and put it aside. Mix the remaining eggs that have been beaten with the garlic, pepper, feta cheese, spinach, and garlic.
2. Unroll pizza dough; roll it into a 12-inch. square. Divide into four squares measuring 6 inches each. Place about one-third of a cup of the spinach mixture on top of each square. After you have folded it into a triangle, squeeze the corners together to seal it. Make slits at the top, then brush with the egg you saved.
3. Place the triangles, if required in batches, in a single layer on the oiled tray that is within the air fryer basket. Cook for 10 to 12 minutes, until the meat, is golden brown. Serve with tzatziki sauce on the side, if desired.

Avocado Cut into Wedge Shapes Wrapped In Bacon

Preparation time: 15 minutes **Cooking time: 25 minutes** **Serving: 2**

Nutrition:

- Calories: 180
- Carbs: 27g
- Protein: 19g
- Fats: 7g

Ingredients

- 2 medium ripe avocados
- 12 bacon strips sauce:
- 1/2 cup mayonnaise
- 1 couple to three teaspoons of Sriracha hot sauce
- 1 to 2 teaspoons of lime juice
- 1 teaspoon grated lime zest

Directions

1. Bring the temperature of the air fryer to 400 degrees. Remove the pit and skin from each avocado, then cut it in half. Divide each of the halves into thirds. Each avocado wedge should have one piece of bacon wrapped around it. If necessary, work in batches to arrange the wedges in a single layer on the tray that is placed within the air fryer basket. Cook for 10 to 15 minutes, or until the bacon is fully cooked.
2. In the meanwhile, combine the mayonnaise, Sriracha sauce, lime juice, and lime zest in a small bowl and whisk to combine. Wedge dishes are best served with sauce.

Zucchini Pizza Fritters

Preparation time: 15 minutes **Cooking time:** 25 minutes **Serving:** 2

Nutrition:

- Calories: 500
- Carbs: 23g
- Protein: 8g
- Fats: 0g

Ingredients

- 2 medium zucchinis
- 1 medium potato, peeled
- 1 small half of an onion
- 1 large egg, lightly beaten
- 2 tablespoons all-purpose flour
- Parmesan cheese, shredded, equal to a half cup
- 1 level teaspoon of powdered garlic
- 1 level teaspoon of powdered onion
- 1/5 of a teaspoon of parsley, in dry flakes
- 1/2 teaspoon salt
- 1 teaspoon pepper

Optional: Marinara sauce, tzatziki sauce, or ranch dressing

Directions

1. Bring the temperature of the air fryer to 400 degrees. Shred the zucchini, potato, and onion into large pieces. Put the grated vegetables on a clean piece of cheesecloth or a tea towel with a double thickness, then gather the corners and squeeze out any excess liquid. Place in a large bowl and whisk in the egg, flour, Parmesan, garlic powder, onion powder, chopped parsley, and a pinch each of salt and pepper. Create patties using a quarter cup of the ingredients.
2. Place the patties, one at a time, in a single layer on the oiled tray that is placed within the air fryer basket. Cook for about 15 to 20 minutes, or until a little browning occurs. If desired, serve with the accompanying sauce.
3. Oven method: Turn the oven on to 400 degrees. Put the fritters on a baking sheet that has been lined with parchment paper. Bake for 15 to 20 minutes, until the bread is golden brown.

Mushroom Roll-Ups Prepared in an Air Fryer

Preparation time: 15 minutes **Cooking time: 25 minutes** **Serving: 2**

Nutrition:

- Calories: 180
- Carbs: 27g
- Protein: 19g
- Fats: 7g

Ingredients

- 2 tablespoons extra virgin olive oil
- 8 ounces of big Portobello mushrooms, with the gills removed and the mushrooms diced finely.
- 1 teaspoon of oregano that has been dried
- 1 teaspoon of thyme in its dry form
- 1/2 milligrams of dried red pepper flakes crushed
- 1/4 teaspoon salt
- 1 container of cream cheese (eight ounces), softened to room temperature
- 4 ounces of ricotta cheese made from whole milk
- 10 flour tortillas (8 inches)
- Cooking spray

Directions

1. In a skillet, heat oil over medium heat. Add mushrooms; sauté 4 minutes. After adding the oregano, thyme, pepper flakes, and salt sauté the mushrooms for 4-6 minutes, or until they have browned. Cool.
2. Combine the cheeses, and then carefully fold in the mushrooms while continuing to combine. On the bottom and middle of each tortilla, spread three tablespoons of the mushroom mixture. Wrap securely in plastic wrap and fasten with toothpicks.
3. Bring the temperature of the air fryer to 400 degrees. Place the roll-ups, one at a time, on a greased tray inside the air fryer basket, and coat them with cooking spray. Cook for 9–11 minutes, until the meat, is golden brown. When the roll-ups are ready to be handled after having cooled, throw away the toothpicks. To accompany, please use chutney.

Thai Meatballs with Chicken

Preparation time: 15 minutes **Cooking time: 25 minutes** **Serving: 2**

Nutrition:

- Calories: 100
- Carbs: 28g
- Protein: 28g
- Fats: 7 g

Ingredients

- 1/2 cup sweet chili sauce
- 2 teaspoons lime juice
- 2 tablespoons ketchup
- 1 tenth of a teaspoon of soy sauce
- 1 big egg, gently beaten
- 3/4 cup panko bread crumbs
- 1 small green onion, cut very finely
- 1 tablespoon of fresh cilantro that has been minced.
- 1/2 teaspoon salt
- 1/2 milligram of the garlic powder
- 1 pound of chicken ground with less fat

Method

1. Bring the temperature of the air fryer to 350 degrees. Mix together the ketchup, chili sauce, lime juice, and soy sauce in a small dish; set aside 1/2 cup of the mixture for serving. Combine the egg, bread crumbs, green onion, cilantro, salt, garlic powder, and the remaining 4 tablespoons of the combination made from chili sauce and cumin in a large bowl. Add in the chicken, and combine it gently but completely. Form into a total of 12 balls.
2. Place the meatballs in the air fryer basket one at a time and put them in a single layer on the oiled tray. Cook for another 4-5 minutes, or until it has a very light brown color. After turning, continue cooking for an additional 4–5 minutes, or until the meat is fully cooked. Serve with the sauce that was saved; top with more chopped cilantro.

Shrimp Cake Sliders Prepared in an Air Fryer

Preparation time: 15 minutes **Cooking time: 20 minutes** **Serving: 2**

Nutrition:

- Calories: 178
- Carbs: 45g
- Protein: 1g
- Fats: 1g

Ingredients

- 1 pound of shrimp, uncooked, peeled, deveined, and numbered between 41 and 50 per pound
- 1 big egg, gently beaten
- 1/2 cup of delicious red pepper that has been coarsely chopped
- 6 green onions, cut and separated into their sections
- 1 tablespoon of fresh gingerroot that has been minced
- 1/4 teaspoon salt
- 1 cup panko breadcrumbs
- 1/4 cup mayonnaise
- 1 teaspoon of Sriracha fiery chili sauce
- 1 teaspoon of mildly sweetened chili sauce
- 5 cups of napa or Chinese cabbage that has been shredded
- 12 tiny buns or dinner rolls, toasted
- 3 tablespoons canola oil
- Additional chili sauce made using Sriracha if desired.

Method

1. Put the shrimp in a food processor and pulse it until it reaches the desired consistency. Egg, red pepper, 4 green onions, ginger, and salt should all be mixed together in a big basin. Mix the shrimp and bread crumbs together in a gentle manner. Form into twelve patties with a thickness of half an inch. Refrigerate for 20 minutes.
2. In the meanwhile, mix the mayonnaise and chili sauces in a large bowl. To this, add the cabbage and the remaining green onions and toss well.
3. Heat the air fryer to 375 degrees. Place the patties, one at a time, in a single layer on the oiled tray that is placed within the air fryer basket. Cook for 8 to 10 minutes, until the meat, is golden brown. Place on buns, top with slaw, and hold together with toothpicks. Serve with more chili sauce on the side, if preferred.

Calamari Prepared in an Air Fryer

Preparation time: 15 minutes **Cooking time: 25 minutes** **Serving: 2**

Nutrition:

- Calories: 140
- Carbs: 25g
- Protein: 14g
- Fats: 6g

Ingredients

- 1/2 cup all-purpose flour
- 1/2 teaspoon salt
- 1 big egg, gently beaten
- 1/2 cup 2% milk
- 1 cup panko breadcrumbs
- 1/2 teaspoon seasoned salt
- 1/4 teaspoon pepper
- 8 ounces of calamari (squid), either fresh or frozen, that has been cleaned, thawed, and sliced into half-inch rings
- Cooking spray

Method

1. Bring the temperature of the air fryer to 400 degrees. Flour and salt should be mixed together in a wide, shallow basin. Whisk the egg and milk together in a separate, shallow basin. Bread crumbs, seasoned salt, and pepper should be mixed together in a third, shallower dish. Prepare the calamari by first coating it in the flour mixture, then dipping it in the egg mixture, and then coating it in the breadcrumb mixture.
2. Spray the calamari with cooking spray and arrange it in a single layer on a tray that has been oiled before placing it in the air fryer basket. Cook for 4 minutes. Flip, then spray with cooking spray. Continue cooking for a further 3–5 minutes, until the meat is golden brown.

Samosas

Preparation time: 15 minutes   **Cooking time: 25 minutes**   **Serving: 2**

Nutrition:

- Calories: 180
- Carbs: 27g
- Protein: 19g
- Fats: 7g

Ingredients

- 2 cups all-purpose flour
- ghee or canola oil, to taste, three teaspoons
- 1/2 teaspoon salt
- a half of a teaspoon's worth of caraway seeds
- 3/4 of a cup of ice water
- 5 medium-sized potatoes, peeled and diced, for the filling
- 6 tablespoons canola oil, split
- 1 cup peas, either fresh or frozen, that have been thawed
- 1 milligram of fresh gingerroot that has been minced
- 1 teaspoon garam masala
- 1/2 milligrams of ground cumin seeds
- 1/2 teaspoon salt

Optional: Caraway seeds, fennel seeds, crushed coriander seeds, and amchur are other options (dried mango powder)

Method

1. Flour, ghee, salt, and caraway seeds should be mixed together in a large basin until the mixture has the consistency of breadcrumbs. Add the water little by little and mix it in until you have a solid dough. Knead the dough for six to eight minutes, or until it is smooth and elastic, after turning it out onto a surface that has been lightly floured. Cover, and let it sit undisturbed for one hour.
2. Put the potatoes in a big saucepan and fill them with water until they are completely submerged. Bring the liquid to a boil. Reduce the heat and continue cooking the vegetables for another 8-10 minutes, then drain. Put to the side to gently cool down. Warm up three tablespoons of oil in a big pan set over a medium flame. After adding the potatoes, continue to cook for about 5 minutes, or until the potatoes begin to adhere to the bottom of the pan. After stirring in the peas, ginger, garam masala, cumin seeds, and salt, continue to simmer for approximately 2 minutes, or until everything is hot. Mix in any of the optional ingredients that you choose. Set aside.
3. Divide dough into 6 pieces. Form one piece of dough into an oval shape about 10 by 6 inches. Divide the dough in half. Apply water along the edge of the straight edge. Form a cone by bringing one of the half corners up to meet the other one of the half corners. To create a seal, pinch the seam. Fill the void with three to four teaspoons of the potato mixture. Apply a thin layer of water along the curved

edge of the dough. Fold the dough over the top of the filling and press to seal the seam. Flatten each samosa by applying a gentle pressing force to the base of each one. Repeat the process with the rest of the dough and filling.

4. Bring the temperature of the air fryer to 350 degrees. Use the remaining three tablespoons of oil to lightly coat each samosa. Arrange the ingredients, one batch at a time, in a single layer on the tray that is placed within the air fryer basket. Cook for approximately 15 minutes, or until the meat is golden brown.

Air-Fryer Spicy Ginger Beef Skewers

Preparation time: 15 minutes **Cooking time: 25 minutes** **Serving: 2**

Nutrition:

- Calories: 100
- Carbs: 28g
- Protein: 28g
- Fats: 7 g

Ingredients

- 1 beef flank steak (1-1/2 pounds)
- 1 cup rice vinegar
- 1 cup soy sauce
- 1/4 cup of brown sugar in its packed form
- 2 tablespoons of minced fresh ginger root
- 6 cloves of garlic, finely chopped
- 3 tablespoons sesame oil
- 1 teaspoon of spicy pepper sauce or 2 tablespoons of Sriracha chili sauce
- Cornstarch, one-half of a teaspoon
- Optional: Green onions that have been cut very thinly and sesame seeds.

Directions

1. Strip the meat to a thickness of one-quarter of an inch. In a large bowl, use a whisk to thoroughly combine the following seven ingredients. A shallow dish should have 1 cup of marinade poured into it. Toss in the meat and flip to coat. Keep covered and chilled for between 2 and 8 hours. Cover and refrigerate leftover marinade.
2. Bring the temperature of the air fryer to 400 degrees. Drain the meat, discarding the marinade in the dish. Skewer the meat on a total of 12 skewers made of metal or wooden skewers that have been soaked in water. Arrange the skewers in a single layer on the oiled tray that is placed within the air fryer basket, working in batches if required. Cook the meat for 4-5 minutes, turning it regularly and basting it often with a half cup of the marinade that was kept until it achieves the doneness that you choose (for medium-rare, a thermometer should register 135°; for medium, 140°; and for medium-well, 145°).
3. In the meanwhile, bring the leftover marinade (about 3/4 cup), which will be used to produce the glaze, to a boil. Whisk in 1/2 teaspoon of cornstarch. Cook for one to two minutes while whisking continuously until the mixture begins to thicken. The glaze should be applied to the skewers just before serving. You may garnish it with chopped green onions and sesame seeds if you want.

Buffalo Bites

Preparation time: 15 minutes **Cooking time: 20 minutes** **Serving: 2**

Nutrition:

- Calories: 140
- Carbs: 25g
- Protein: 14g
- Fats: 6g

Ingredients

- 1 small head of cauliflower, separated into florets and cut into pieces
- 2 tablespoons olive oil
- a tablespoon and a half of Buffalo wing sauce
- 3 tablespoons butter, melted dip:
- 1-1/2 cups 2% cottage cheese
- 1/4 cup of plain Greek yogurt that is fat-free
- 1/4 cup of blue cheese in crushed form
- 1 envelope ranch salad dressing mix
- Sticks of celery, as an alternative

Method

1. Bring the temperature of the air fryer to 350 degrees. Cauliflower and oil should be mixed together in a large basin and then tossed to coat. Prepare the cauliflower for the air fryer by layering it in a single layer, batch after batch. Cook for about 10 to 15 minutes, stirring once halfway through until the florets are soft, and the edges are browned.
2. The Buffalo sauce and the melted butter should be mixed together in a big basin. Add cauliflower, then mix to coat everything evenly. Place on a dish intended for serving. Put all of the ingredients for the dip into a small dish. Serve the dish with cauliflower and celery sticks on the side, if preferred.

Air-Fryer French Fries

Preparation time: 15 minutes **Cooking time: 25 minutes** **Serving: 2**

Nutrition:

- Calories: 180
- Carbs: 27g
- Protein: 19g
- Fats: 7g

Ingredients

- 3 medium potatoes, sliced into 1/2-inch slices
- 2 tablespoons coconut or avocado oil
- 1/2 milligram of the garlic powder
- 1/4 teaspoon salt
- 1/4 teaspoon pepper
- Optional fresh parsley that has been chopped

Method

1. Bring the temperature of the air fryer to 400 degrees. Place potatoes in a big basin and pour cold water over them until they are covered. Soak for 15 minutes. After draining the potatoes, lay them on paper towels and pat them dry.
2. In a second large bowl, combine the potatoes, oil, garlic powder, salt, and pepper; then toss to combine and coat. In stages, arrange potatoes in a single layer on the tray and insert them in the oiled basket of the air fryer. Cook for 15–17 minutes, tossing and rotating the food every 5-7 minutes until it reaches a golden brown and crisp consistency. Add some chopped parsley on top, if you want.

Air-Fryer Spring Rolls with a Crispy Sriracha Sauce

Preparation time: 15 minutes　　**Cooking time: 25 minutes**　　**Serving: 2**

Nutrition:

- Calories: 500
- Carbs: 23g
- Protein: 8g
- Fats: 0g

Ingredients

- 3 cups coleslaw mix (about 7 ounces)
- 3 finely chopped green onions
- 1 tablespoon soy sauce
- 1 teaspoon sesame oil
- Breasts of boneless, skinless chicken weighing one pound
- 1 teaspoon seasoned salt
- 2 bundles (8 ounces each) of cream cheese that have been softened
- 2 tablespoons Sriracha chili sauce
- 24 wrappers for spring rolls.
- Cooking spray

Optional: Sweet chili sauce, in addition to the added scallions

Method

1. Bring the temperature of the air fryer to 360 degrees. Toss together the coleslaw mix, green onions, soy sauce, and sesame oil, and then set aside while the chicken is cooking. In the basket of an air fryer, arrange the chicken pieces in a single layer on a greased surface. Cook the chicken for 18 to 20 minutes, or until a thermometer inserted into the bird registers 165 degrees. Remove the chicken and let it gently cool. After the chicken has been finely chopped, combine it with the seasoned salt.
2. Raise the temperature of the air fryer to 400 degrees. Blend the cream cheese and Sriracha chili sauce together in a large bowl, then add in the combination of chicken and coleslaw. Place roughly two teaspoons worth of filling directly below the middle of a spring roll wrapper, with one of the corners of the wrapper facing you. (Until you are ready to use the wrappers, cover any that are left over with a moist paper towel.) The bottom corner should be folded over the filling, and the remaining edges should be moistened with water. Fold the side corners in toward the center over the filling, then roll the filling up firmly while pushing the tip to seal it. Repeat.
3. Arrange the spring rolls in a single layer on a greased tray inside the air fryer basket, and then spray them with cooking spray. Do this in batches. Cook for another 5 or 6 minutes, until it has a very light brown colour. Flip, then spray with with cooking spray. Continue cooking for a further 5-6 minutes, or until the bacon is crisp and golden brown. You may serve this dish with sweet chili sauce and top it with chopped green onions, if you want.

Air-Fryer Fiesta Chicken Fingers

Preparation time: 10 minutes **Cooking time: 15 minutes** **Serving: 1**

Nutrition:

- Calories: 180
- Carbs: 27g
- Protein: 19g
- Fats: 7g

Ingredients

- Breasts of boneless, skinless chicken weighing a total of 0.7 pounds
- 1 half a cup of buttermilk
- 1/4 teaspoon pepper
- 1 cup all-purpose flour
- a total of three cups of corn chips, crushed
- 1 packet of taco seasoning in an envelope
- Cream Fraiche ranch dip or salsa

Method

1. Bring the temperature of the air fryer to 400 degrees. Use a meat mallet to achieve a thickness of half an inch in the chicken breasts. Strips with a width of 1 inch should be cut.
2. Buttermilk and black pepper should be whisked together in a small basin. Put the flour in a second basin that is shallower. In a third dish, combine the corn chips and taco seasoning and mix well. Coat the chicken in flour on both sides, then brush off any excess flour. First, coat in the buttermilk mixture then transfers to the corn chip mixture and pat to help the coating stick.
3. Arrange the chicken in a single layer on a tray that has been coated and placed inside the air fryer basket. Spritz the chicken with cooking spray. Cook the chicken for 7-8 minutes on each side, or until the coating is golden brown and the chicken is no longer pink. Continue in this manner with the remaining chicken. Served with ranch dip or salsa as an accompaniment.

Air-Fryer Cheeseburger Onion Rings

Preparation time: 15 minutes   **Cooking time:** 25 minutes   **Serving:** 2

Nutrition:

- Calories: 500
- Carbs: 23g
- Protein: 8g
- Fats: 0g

Ingredients

- 1 pound of lean ground beef, which is at least 90% lean.
- 1/3 cup ketchup
- 2 teaspoons prepared mustard
- 1/2 teaspoon salt
- 1 substantial onion
- 4 ounces of squarely cut cheddar cheese, sliced into 8 pieces.
- 3/4 cup all-purpose flour
- 2 teaspoons of dried minced garlic
- 2 big eggs, gently beaten
- 1-1/2 cups panko breadcrumbs
- Cooking spray
- Ketchup with a kick, if desired.

Method

1. Bring the temperature of the air fryer to 335 degrees. Mix the ground beef, ketchup, mustard and salt together in a small bowl until everything is evenly distributed. Slice the onion to a thickness of half an inch, then divide it into rings. Place a quarter of the beef mixture on each of the eight slices (save the remaining onion rings for another use). On top of each, place a piece of cheese, and then spread the leftover meat mixture over the top.
2. Flour and garlic powder should be mixed together in a small basin. Separate eggs, bread crumbs, and eggs into separate basins of a similar shallow depth. Rings of stuffed onion shake off any extra flour after being dipped in flour to cover both sides. After dipping in egg, coat with bread crumbs and push down to help the coating stick.
3. Place the onion rings, one batch at a time, in a single layer on the greased tray that is within the air fryer basket. Spritz the onion rings with cooking spray. Cook for 12 to 15 minutes, until it reaches a golden-brown color and a thermometer placed into the meat registers 160 degrees. Serve with spicy ketchup on the side, if preferred.

Garlic-Rosemary Brussels Sprouts Prepared in an Air Fryer

Preparation time: 15 minutes **Cooking time: 25 minutes** **Serving: 2**

Nutrition:

- Calories: 140
- Carbs: 25g
- Protein: 14g
- Fats: 6g

Ingredients

- 3 tablespoons olive oil
- 2 cloves of garlic, finely chopped
- 1/2 teaspoon salt
- a quarter of a teaspoon of pepper
- 1 pound of Brussels sprouts, which have been cleaned, halved and trimmed.
- 1/2 cup panko breadcrumbs
- 1-and-a-half milligrams of fresh rosemary, minced

Methods

1. Bring the temperature of the air fryer to 350 degrees. Put the first four ingredients into a small dish that is appropriate for the microwave, and then heat them for 30 seconds at high power.
2. Toss the Brussels sprouts with the oil combination that has been measured out to be 2 teaspoons. Cook the Brussels sprouts for four to five minutes after placing them on a tray in the air fryer basket. Sprouts to be stirred. Continue to boil the sprouts for about 8 more minutes, stirring once halfway through the cooking period, until they have a light brown color and are almost at the required softness.
3. Combine the breadcrumbs, rosemary, and the rest of the oil mixture in a bowl, and then sprinkle it over the sprouts. Continue to heat for a further 3–5 minutes, or until the crumbs are browned and the sprouts are soft. Immediately serve after cooking.

Quinoa Arancini Prepared with an Air Fryer

Preparation time: 15 minutes **Cooking time: 25 minutes** **Serving: 2**

Nutrition:

- Calories: 178
- Carbs: 45g
- Protein: 1g
- Fats: 1g

Ingredients

- 1 package (9 ounces) of ready-to-serve quinoa or 1-3/4 cups of cooked quinoa
- Use 2 big eggs that have been softly beaten and then split.
- 1 cup of breadcrumbs that have been seasoned, divided
- 1 tablespoon and a quarter of grated Parmesan cheese
- 1 tablespoon olive oil
- 2 teaspoons of dried basil or 2 tablespoons of minced fresh basil
- 1/2 milligram of the garlic powder
- 1/2 teaspoon salt
- 1/8 teaspoon pepper
- 6 cubes of mozzarella cheese with a partial skim, each measuring 3/4 inches.

Methods

1. Heat the air fryer to 375 degrees. Prepare the quinoa in accordance with the instructions on the box. Mix in one egg, half a cup of breadcrumbs, and one ounce of grated Parmesan cheese, olive oil, basil, and spices.
2. Divide into 6 parts. Form a ball by rolling each part around a cheese cube until it is fully covered, then set it aside.
3. Put the remaining egg and half a cup of breadcrumbs in two separate dishes of a similar depth. After coating in egg, quinoa balls should be rolled in breadcrumbs. Place the food in the air fryer basket on a greased tray, then coat it with cooking spray. Cook for 6 to 8 minutes, until the meat, is golden brown. Serve the pasta with sauce on the side, if preferred.

Air-Fried Meatballs Stuffed with Figs and Goat Cheese

Preparation time: 15 minutes **Cooking time: 25 to 30 minutes** **Serving: 2**

Nutrition:

- Calories: 100
- Carbs: 28g
- Protein: 28g
- Fats: 7 g

Ingredients

- 1/2 cup panko breadcrumbs
- 1 big egg, beaten using very little force.
- 1 pound bulk Italian sausage
- two and a half ounces of fresh goat cheese
- 1/2 cup of vinegar made from red wine
- 1/4 cup sugar
- a single stick of cinnamon (3 inches)
- 2 whole cloves of garlic
- 1 complete seed of star anise
- half a cup of chopped dried figs
- half a cup of water

Method

1. Bring the temperature of the air fryer to 350 degrees. Breadcrumbs and eggs should be mixed together in a big basin. Add the sausage and mix it in gently but completely. Divide into 18 parts. Form each part around a half teaspoon of cheese, making sure it is well covered. The meatballs should be placed on a greased tray in the air fryer basket in batches. Cook for another 25 to 30 minutes until everything is thoroughly cooked.

2. During this time, put the vinegar, sugar, cinnamon, cloves, and star anise into a large saucepan and bring them to a boil. Turn the heat down; simmer for another five minutes. Cinnamon, cloves, and star anise should be thrown away. Add the figs and simmer for another 8-10 minutes, or until they have become softer. Take the pan off the heat and let it cool slightly. Transfer to a blender. Process until almost completely smooth after adding a half cup of water. To serve, add meatballs to the dish. If you want, you may sprinkle some chopped chives on top of the meatballs.

Empanadas

Preparation time: 15 minutes **Cooking time: 25 minutes** **Serving: 2**

Nutrition:

- Calories: 178
- Carbs: 45g
- Protein: 1g
- Fats: 1g

Ingredients

- 1 tablespoon olive oil
- 1 medium-sized sweet onion, cut in half and sliced very thinly
- 1 fresh goat cheese log, crumbled, weighing about 4 ounces
- 1/4 cup sun-dried tomatoes that have been coarsely chopped and packed in oil; drain the tomatoes
- Dough for a pie with a single crust or one sheet of pre-made pie crust from the refrigerator
- Cooking spray

Methods

1. In a large skillet, heat oil over medium heat. Add the onion and continue to cook and stir it for another 4-5 minutes until it has softened. Turn the temperature down to medium-low. Cook for 30 to 40 minutes, stirring the mixture regularly until it reaches a deep golden-brown color. Take the pan off the heat. Let it come to room temperature. Mix in the goat cheese and tomatoes with a light hand.
2. Heat the air fryer to 375 degrees. On a surface that has been dusted with flour, roll out the dough to a thickness of 14 inches. Use a biscuit cutter with a diameter of 3 inches that has been dusted with flour. Put one heaping teaspoonful of filling on the bottom half of each round. Coat the pastry edges with water and fold the circles in half to make triangles. Press the edges together using a fork to seal them.
3. When using the air fryer, put the empanadas in a single layer on a greased tray that is placed within the basket, and then coat the tray with cooking spray. After around four to five minutes, the food should be golden brown. Flip, then spray with cooking spray. Continue cooking for a further 4–5 minutes, until the meat is golden brown.

Components of an Air-Fried Ravioli Dish

Preparation time: 15 minutes **Cooking time: 25 minutes** **Serving: 2**

Nutrition:

- Calories: 180
- Carbs: 27g
- Protein: 19g
- Fats: 7g

Ingredients

- 1 cup of breadcrumbs that have been seasoned.
- 1 tablespoon and a quarter of grated Parmesan cheese
- 2 tablespoons dried basil
- 1/2 cup all-purpose flour
- 2 big eggs, gently beaten
- 1 thawed bag of frozen ravioli with meat filling (nine ounces).
- Cooking spray
- Optional fresh minced basil served fresh
- 1 cup marinara sauce, warmed

Methods

1. Bring the temperature of the air fryer to 350 degrees. Combine the breadcrumbs, Parmesan cheese, and basil in a basin of shallow depth. Put the flour on the bottom of one shallow dish, then the eggs on the other. After coating, both sides of the ravioli with flour, brush off any excess flour. First, coat in egg, then press into crumb mixture; this will help the coating stick.
2. When using the air fryer, place the ravioli in a single layer on a greased tray and then spray it with cooking spray. Do this in batches. Cook for another 3–4 minutes, or until the meat is golden brown. Flip, then spray with cooking spray. Continue cooking for a further 3–4 minutes, until the meat is golden brown. If you so wish, immediately top the dish with extra basil and Parmesan cheese. Warm it up and serve it with marinara sauce.

Air-Fryer Taquitos

Preparation time: 10 minutes **Cooking time: 20 minutes** **Serving: 2**

Nutrition:

- Calories: 500
- Carbs: 23g
- Protein: 8g
- Fats: 0g

Ingredients

- 2 big eggs
- 1/2 cup of breadcrumbs that are dry
- 1 packet of taco seasoning, 3 teaspoons
- 1 pound of lean ground beef, which is at least 90% lean.
- 10 warmed corn tortillas, each about 6 inches in diameter
- Cooking spray
- Optional: Salsa with guacamole

Methods

1. Bring the temperature of the air fryer to 350 degrees. Eggs, breadcrumbs, and taco spice should be mixed together in a large basin. Add the meat and mix it softly but completely.
2. Place a heaping tablespoonful of the meat mixture in the middle of each tortilla. Roll up firmly, and then use toothpicks to fasten the roll. Arrange the taquitos in a single layer on a tray that has been greased and placed inside the air fryer basket. Spritz the tray with cooking spray. Cook for 6 minutes, then flip and continue cooking for another 6-7 minutes, until the taquitos are golden brown and crispy, and the meat is fully cooked through. Before serving, you should throw away the toothpicks. Serve with salsa and guacamole on the side, if desired.

Air-Fried Cauliflower

Preparation time: 10 minutes **Cooking time: 15 minutes** **Serving: 1**

Nutrition:

- Calories: 180
- Carbs: 27g
- Protein: 19g
- Fats: 7g

Ingredients

- 1/2 cup all-purpose flour
- 1 half a cup of cornstarch and one teaspoon of salt
- 1 teaspoon baking powder
- 3/4 cup club soda
- 1 medium-sized head of cauliflower, broken up into florets measuring 1 inch (about 6 cups)
- **Sauce:**
- 1/4 cup orange juice
- 3 tablespoons sugar
- 3 tablespoons soy sauce
- 3 tablespoons vegetable broth
- 2 tablespoons rice vinegar
- 2 tablespoons sesame oil
- cornstarch equivalent to 2 tablespoons
- 2 tablespoons canola oil
- 2 to 6 dried pasilla peppers or other types of fiery chilies, chopped 2 to 3 green onions, with the white parts minced and the green parts cut very thinly
- three cloves of garlic, minced
- 1 milligram of finely grated fresh ginger root
- 1/2 milligrams of orange zest that has been granted.
- 4 cups of simmered and piping hot rice

Methods

1. Bring the temperature of the air fryer to 400 degrees. Mix together the dry ingredients (flour, cornstarch, salt, and baking powder). Mix in the club soda until it is completely incorporated (the batter will be thin). Toss the florets in the batter, and then place them on a wire rack that has been placed over a baking sheet. Let stand for 5 minutes. Cauliflower should be placed in the air fryer basket in batches, on a greased tray. 10 to 12 minutes, or until the meat is golden brown and tender.
2. In the meanwhile, mix together the first six sauce components before adding the cornstarch and continuing to whisk until smooth.
3. The canola oil should be heated in a large saucepan over medium-high heat. After adding the chilies, continue cooking while stirring them for another one to two minutes. Cook for approximately a minute, or until the onions' white parts, garlic, ginger, and orange zest start to release their aromas. Stir orange juice mixture; add to saucepan. Bring to a boil, then continue to simmer and whisk for another 2–4 minutes until the mixture has thickened.

4. To the sauce, add the cauliflower, and toss to coat. Serve over rice and top with green onions that have been cut very thinly.

Nashville Hot Chicken Prepared in an Air Fryer

Preparation time: 15 minutes **Cooking time: 25 minutes** **Serving: 2**

Nutrition:

- Calories: 100
- Carbs: 28g
- Protein: 28g
- Fats: 7 g

Ingredients

- Split amounts of 2 tablespoons of dill pickle juice, 2 tablespoons of spicy pepper sauce, and 1 teaspoon of salt
- 2 pounds of chicken tenderloins
- 1 cup all-purpose flour
- 1 half of a teaspoon of pepper
- 1 big egg
- half a cup of buttermilk
- Cooking spray
- 1/2 cup olive oil
- 2 tbsp. cayenne pepper
- 2 tablespoons sugar in its dark brown form
- 1 teaspoon paprika
- 1 teaspoon of ground chili peppers
- 1/2 milligram of the garlic powder
- Dill pickle slices

Methods

1. Combine one tablespoon of pickle juice, one tablespoon of spicy sauce, and half a teaspoon of salt in a bowl or other container with a shallow depth. After adding the chicken, toss to coat. Refrigerate while covered for at least one hour before serving. After draining the chicken, throw away any marinade that was used.
2. Heat the air fryer to 375 degrees. Flour, the remaining half of the teaspoon of salt, and pepper should be mixed together in a basin that is not too deep. Egg, buttermilk, and the remaining 1 tablespoon of pickle juice and 1 tablespoon of spicy sauce should be whisked together in a separate, shallow dish. Coat the chicken in flour on both sides, then brush off any excess flour. First, dunk in the egg mixture, and then proceed to the flour mixture.
3. Arrange the chicken in a single layer on a tray that has been thoroughly oiled and place it in the air fryer basket. Spritz the chicken with cooking spray. Cook for another 5 or 6 minutes, until the meat, is golden brown. Flip, then spray with cooking spray. Continue to cook for a further 5–6 minutes, until the meat is golden brown.
4. Mix the next six ingredients together with a whisk, then pour them over the heated chicken and toss to coat. Accompany the meal with pickles.

Beef Wellington Wontons Prepared in an Air Fryer

Preparation time: 15 minutes **Cooking time: 25 minutes** **Serving: 2**

Nutrition:

- Calories: 178
- Carbs: 45g
- Protein: 1g
- Fats: 1g

Ingredients

- 1 half pound of lean ground beef that is at least 90% lean.
- 1 single teaspoon of butter
- 1 tablespoon olive oil
- 2 cloves of garlic, finely chopped
- 1-and-a-half milligrams of chopped shallot
- 1 cup of chopped fresh shiitake mushrooms, 1 cup of baby portobello mushrooms, and 1 cup of white mushrooms
- 1 quarter of a cup of dry red wine
- 1 tablespoon of fresh parsley that has been minced
- 1/2 teaspoon salt
- a quarter of a teaspoon of pepper
- 1 packet of wonton wrappers weighing 12 ounces
- 1 big egg
- 1 teaspoon of water in total
- Cooking spray

Methods

1. Bring the temperature of the air fryer to 325 degrees. Cook the beef in a small pan over medium heat until it is no longer pink, about 4-5 minutes, and then crumble it. Move the mixture to a big bowl. Butter and olive oil should be heated together in the same pan over medium-high heat. Cook for one minute after adding the garlic and shallot. Mix in the mushrooms, then add the wine. Cook for another 8-10 minutes, or until the mushrooms are soft, and then add them to the meat. Mix in some parsley, as well as some salt and pepper.

2. In the middle of each wonton wrapper, distribute roughly 2 tablespoons worth of the filling. Whisk together the egg and the water. The egg mixture should be used to moisten the sides of the wonton. Fold opposing corners over the filling and press to close.

3. Wontons should be arranged in a single layer and sprayed with cooking spray before being placed in the air fryer basket. This should be done in batches. Cook for another 4-5 minutes, or until it has a very light brown color. Flip, then spray with cooking spray. Continue cooking for a further 4-5 minutes, until the bacon is crisp and golden brown. To be served hot.

Air Fryer Pumpkin Fries

Preparation time: 15 minutes **Cooking time: 25 minutes** **Serving: 2**

Nutrition:

- Calories: 180
- Carbs: 27g
- Protein: 19g
- Fats: 7g

Ingredients

- 1/2 cup of Greek yogurt in its plain form
- 2 tablespoons maple syrup
- Between two and three tablespoons of minced chipotle chiles that have been marinated in adobo sauce
- 1/8 teaspoon + 1/2 teaspoon salt, split
- 1 medium pie pumpkin
- 1/4 milligram of the garlic powder
- 1 quarter of milligrams of cumin powder
- 1 quarter of a teaspoon of chili powder
- 1 quarter of a teaspoon of pepper

Methods

1. Yogurt, maple syrup, chipotle peppers, and an eighth of a teaspoon of salt should be mixed together in a small basin. Refrigerate, covered, until serving.
2. Bring the temperature of the air fryer to 400 degrees. The pumpkin should be peeled and then sliced in half lengthwise. Throw away the seeds or preserve them to toast later. The pumpkin should be sliced into strips of half an inch. Move the mixture to a big bowl. Mix in the remaining half of a teaspoon of salt, along with the garlic powder, cumin, chili powder, and pepper. Toss to evenly distribute the seasonings.
3. The pumpkin should be arranged on a greased tray and placed in the air fryer basket in batches. Cook until barely tender, 6-8 minutes. To disperse the ingredients, give them a toss, and continue cooking them for three to five minutes more. Include sauce on the plate.

Hot Meatballs Prepared in an Air Fryer

Preparation time: 15 minutes **Cooking time: 20 minutes** **Serving: 2**

Nutrition:

- Calories: 140
- Carbs: 25g
- Protein: 14g
- Fats: 6g

Ingredients

- 2/3 cup oats suitable for rapid preparation
- 1/2 cup of Ritz crackers that have been crushed
- 2 big eggs, beaten with very little water
- 1 can of evaporated milk (five ounces total)
- 1 teaspoon of dried onion that has been minced
- 1 teaspoon salt
- 1 level teaspoon of powdered garlic
- 1 teaspoon of cumin that has been ground
- 1 milligram (mg) of honey
- half of a teaspoon of pepper
- 2 pounds of lean ground beef, which is at least 90% lean.

Sauce:

- 1/3 cup of brown sugar in its packed form
- 13 of a cup of honey
- 1/3 cup orange marmalade
- Cornstarch equivalent to 2 teaspoons
- 2 teaspoons soy sauce
- 1 to 2 tablespoons Louisiana-style spicy sauce
- 1 teaspoonful of Worcestershire sauce

Methods

1. Bring the temperature of the air fryer to 380 degrees. Put the first ten ingredients into a large bowl and mix them together. Add the meat and mix it softly but completely. Form into balls with a diameter of 1 1/2 inches.
2. Place the meatballs in the air fryer basket one at a time and put them in a single layer on the oiled tray. Cook them for 12 to 15 minutes, or until they have a light brown color on the outside and are fully cooked within. In the meanwhile, put all of the sauce ingredients in a small pot. Cook while stirring over a heat setting medium until the mixture has thickened. To serve, add meatballs to the cisn.

Mini Chimichangas Prepared in an Air Fryer

Preparation time: 15 minutes **Cooking time: 25 minutes** **Serving: 2**

Nutrition:

- Calories: 178
- Carbs: 45g
- Protein: 1g
- Fats: 1g

Ingredients

- 1 kilogram of minced beef
- 1 diced onion of medium size
- 1 packet of taco seasoning in an envelope
- 1/4 of a cup of water
- Three cups of shredded Monterey jack cheese Cheddar with jack
- 1 cup sour cream
- 1 can (4 ounces) (4 ounces) green chiles, chopped, with the liquid drained off
- 14 wonton wrappers for egg rolls
- 1 big egg white, beaten with just a little bit of salt
- Cooking spray
- Salsa

Methods

1. Cook the beef and onion together in a large pan over medium heat until the beef is no longer pink; shred the cooked pieces and drain. Mix in the taco spice along with the water. Bring the liquid to a boil. Turn the heat down and let the mixture simmer, uncovered, for five minutes while stirring it periodically. Take the pan off the heat and let it cool slightly.
2. Heat the air fryer to 375 degrees. Mix the cheese, sour cream, and chopped chilies together in a large basin. Mix in the ground beef mixture. Position a corner of the egg roll wrapper so that it is facing you when it is placed in the work area. Put about a third of a cup of the filling in the middle. After folding in the sides, fold the bottom one-third of the wrapper over the filling.
3. Coat the tip at the top with egg white, then wrap it up to seal it. Repeat the process with the rest of the wrappers and the filling. (To prevent the leftover egg roll wrappers from drying out, keep them covered with waxed paper.)
4. Chimichangas should be arranged in a single layer and sprayed with cooking spray while they are placed in the air fryer basket in batches. Cook for three to four minutes on each side, or until golden brown. Serve while still heated with more sour cream and salsa on the side.

Beefy Swiss Bundles Prepared in an Air Fryer

Preparation time: 10 minutes **Cooking time: 15 minutes** **Serving: 1**

Nutrition:

- Calories: 100
- Carbs: 28g
- Protein: 28g
- Fats: 7 g

Ingredients

- 1 kilogram of minced beef
- 1-and-a-half cups of fresh mushrooms that have been sliced
- 1/4 of a cup of minced onion
- 1-and-a-half tablespoons of garlic, minced
- Worcestershire sauce, to taste, four tablespoons
- 3/4 of a crushed teaspoon of rosemary that has been dried.
- 3/4 teaspoon paprika
- 1/2 teaspoon salt
- 1 quarter of a teaspoon of pepper
- 1 defrosted sheet of puff pastry from the freezer
- 2/3 cup of mashed potatoes that have been chilled
- Swiss cheese, shredded, equaling one cup
- 1 big egg
- 2 measuring spoons of water

Method

1. Heat the air fryer to 375 degrees. Cook the beef, mushrooms, and onion in a large pan over medium heat for about 8 to 10 minutes, or until the meat is no longer pink and the veggies are soft. Crumble the cooked beef. Cook for a further minute after adding the garlic. Drain. Mix in the Worcestershire sauce as well as the other ingredients. Take the pan from the heat and place it to the side.
2. On a surface dusted with flour, lay out the puff pastry into a rectangle measuring 15 by 13 inches. Rectangular pieces measuring 7-1/2 by 6-1/2 inches should be cut out. Spread about two tablespoons of potatoes on each rectangle and do so to within one inch of the edges. Place three-quarters of a cup of the meat mixture on top of each, then sprinkle with a quarter cup of cheese.
3. Whisk together the egg and water, then brush the wash down the pastry's edges. Place the opposite corners of the pastry over each bundle, then squeeze the seams together to seal them. Coat with the remaining egg mixture and brush. Place the pastries, one at a time, in a single layer on the tray that is within the air fryer basket. Cook for 10 to 12 minutes, or until golden brown.

Air-Fried Drumsticks with a Crispy Curry Finish

Preparation time: 15 minutes **Cooking time: 25 minutes** **Serving: 2**

Nutrition:

- Calories:140
- Carbs: 25g
- Protein: 14g
- Fats: 6g

Ingredients

- 1 pound chicken drumsticks
- 3/4 teaspoon salt, split
- 2 tablespoons olive oil
- curry powder equivalent to 2 tablespoons
- 1/2 teaspoon onion salt
- 1/2 milligram of the garlic powder
- Minced fresh cilantro, as an alternative

Directions

1. Put the chicken in a big bowl, and season it with half a teaspoon of salt and as much water as is needed to cover it. Allow standing at room temperature for fifteen minutes. Drain, then dry with a towel.
2. Heat the air fryer to 375 degrees. In a separate dish, combine the remaining 1/4 teaspoon of salt with the curry powder, onion salt, and garlic powder. Add the oil, and then add the chicken and toss to coat. Place chicken in an even layer on a tray and place it in the air fryer's basket in batches. 15–17 minutes total, turning the chicken once halfway through cooking until a thermometer inserted into the chicken reads 170–175 degrees Fahrenheit. Add some chopped cilantro on top, if you like.

Index:

AIR FRIED TERIYAKI PORK CHOPS; 56
Air Fryer BBQ Chicken Wings; 63
Air Fryer Breakfast Sweet Potato Skins; 17
Air Fryer Broccoli; 46
Air Fryer Brussels sprouts; 47
Air Fryer Donuts; 12
Air Fryer Honey Garlic Chicken Wings; 58
Air Fryer Honey Mustard Salmon; 72
Air Fryer Pumpkin Fries; 110
Air Fryer Steak Kabobs; 76
Air Fryer Swai Fish; 60
Air-Fried Cauliflower; 106
Air-Fried Chicken Fajitas in the Air Fryer; 57
Air-Fried Drumsticks with a Crispy Curry Finish; 114
Air-Fried Ham and Egg Pockets in the Air Fryer; 23
Air-Fried Meatballs Stuffed with Figs and Goat Cheese; 102
Air-Fried Spinach and Feta; 85
Air-Fryer Cheeseburger Onion Rings; 99
Air-Fryer Chicken Wings; 82
Air-Fryer Fiesta Chicken Fingers; 98
Air-Fryer French Fries; 96
Air-Fryer Red Potatoes; 27
Air-Fryer Shrimp in a Sauce Made of Coconut and Apricots; 84
Air-Fryer Spicy Ginger Beef Skewers; 94
Air-Fryer Spring Rolls with a Crispy Sriracha Sauce; 97
Air-Fryer Taquitos; 105
Apple Fritters Prepared with an Air Fryer; 9
Avocado Cut into Wedge Shapes Wrapped In Bacon; 86
Baby Back Ribs Cooked in an Air Fryer; 53
Beef Wellington Wontons Prepared in an Air Fryer; 109
Beefy Swiss Bundles Prepared in an Air Fryer; 113
Bourbon bacon cooked in an air fryer; 25
Breaded Pork Chops Cooked in an Air Fryer; 55
Broccoli cheese soup; 33
Buffalo Bites; 95
Buffalo Chicken Wings Baked In the Air Fryer; 66
Cajun Air Fryer Salmon Two salmon fillets; 49
Calamari Prepared in an Air Fryer; 91
Candied Bacon Finished In the Air Fryer; 19
Catfish cooked in an air fryer; 74
Caviar; 32
Cheesy Breakfast Egg Rolls; 20
Chicken Breasts Prepared in an Air Fryer; 77
Chicken Parmesan; 64
Chicken Prepared In an Air Fryer; 71
Chicken Street Tacos Made In the Air Fryer; 68
Chickpea Tot Hot dish; 37
Components of an Air-Fried Ravioli Dish; 104
Cookies Prepared with an Air Fryer; 18
Crepes that Have Been Folded, Filled with Smoked Ham, and Topped with Butter; 40
Crispy Breakfast Burritos Prepared in an Air Fryer; 10
Croquettes for breakfast made in the air fryer with eggs and asparagus; 16
Cups of French toast cooked in an air fryer, topped with raspberries; 14
Empanadas; 103
Garlic Bread Prepared in an Air Fryer; 83
Garlic-Rosemary Brussels Sprouts Prepared in an Air Fryer; 100
Hawaiian Plate Lunch with Macaroni Salad; 45
Homemade Chicken Apple Sausage; 34
Hot Meatballs Prepared in an Air Fryer; 11
Kid-Friendly Pizzadillas; 43
Lobster Tails for the Air Fryer; 62
Meatloaf; 54
Mexican-Style Stuffed Chicken Breasts Prepared in an Air Fryer; 50
Mini Chimichangas Prepared in an Air Fryer; 112
Mini Nutella Doughnut Holes Made with an Air Fryer; 24
Mushroom Roll-Ups Prepared in an Air Fryer; 88
Nachos Prepared in an Air Fryer; 75
Nashville Hot Chicken Prepared in an Air Fryer; 108
Open "Face" Egg Salad Sandwiches; 41
Parmesan-Crusted Chicken Done In the Air Fryer; 69
Pickles Prepared in an Air Fryer; 81
Pimiento Grilled Cheese; 42
Pistachio-Crusted Chicken Prepared in an Air Fryer; 70
Pork Chops Cooked In an Air Fryer; 79
Puff Pastry Danishes Baked in an Air Fryer; 28
Quick BBQ Sausage Sloppy Joes; 39
Quinoa Arancini Prepared with an Air Fryer; 101
Ribeye Steak; 61
Salad made with creamy chicken; 44
Samosas; 92
Scotch Eggs Prepared in an Air Fryer; 15
Shrimp Cake Sliders Prepared in an Air Fryer; 90
Sticks of French toast cooked in an air fryer; 26
Taco Casserole Made In the Air Fryer; 73
Thai Meatballs with Chicken; 89
The Banana Bread Pizza Made In the Air Fryer; 21
The Ultimate Spinach and Artichoke Dip; 30
The Very Best Cinnamon Rolls; 35
Turkey Breast Prepared in an Air Fryer; 52
Zucchini Pizza Fritters; 87

Conclusion

cooking your meals in an air fryer may be more beneficial to your health than using other methods. The device may assist you in controlling your weight and lowering your exposure to potentially harmful chemicals and substances that may be produced when meals are deep-fried. Be sure to read the directions before beginning to ensure that your food is cooked properly and that you can enjoy the advantages of using an air fryer.

Made in United States
Orlando, FL
05 February 2023